the **red hot chile**
cookbook

the **red hot chile**
cookbook   Fabulously fiery recipes for chile fans

Dan May

photography by Peter Cassidy

RYLAND
PETERS
& SMALL

LONDON NEW YORK

Design and Photographic Art Direction Steve Painter
Commissioning Editor Céline Hughes
Production Manager Gordana Simakovic
Art Director Leslie Harrington
Editorial Director Julia Charles

Food Stylist Lizzie Harris
Prop Stylist Róisín Neild
Indexer Penelope Kent

First published in 2012 by
Ryland Peters & Small
20–21 Jockey's Fields
London WC1R 4BW
and
519 Broadway, 5th Floor
New York, NY 10012
www.rylandpeters.com

10 9 8 7 6 5 4 3 2 1

All photography by Peter Cassidy except
pages 7, 9, 11–13 and 15 by Dan May.

Text © Dan May 2012
Design and photographs
© Ryland Peters & Small 2012

Printed in China

UK ISBN: 978 1 84975 222 0
US ISBN: 978 1 84975 224 4

A CIP record for this book is available from
the British Library.

A CIP record for this book is available from
the Library of Congress.

Notes

• The recipes in this book are given in both metric
and imperial measurements. However, the
spellings are primarily British and this includes
all terminology relating to chilli peppers. British
'chilli' and 'chillies' are used where Americans
would use 'chile', 'chili' and 'chiles'.
• All spoon measurements are level, unless
otherwise specified.
• All chillies are fresh unless otherwise stated.
• All eggs are medium (UK) or large (US), unless
otherwise specified. Uncooked or partially
cooked eggs should not be served to the very
young, the very old, those with compromised
immune systems, or to pregnant women.
• When a recipe calls for the grated zest of citrus
fruit, buy unwaxed fruit and wash well before
use. If you can only find treated fruit, scrub well
in warm soapy water and rinse before using.
• Ovens should be preheated to the specified
temperature. Recipes in this book were tested
using a regular oven. If using a fan/convection
oven, follow the manufacturer's instructions for
adjusting temperatures.
• Sterilize preserving jars before use. Wash them
in hot, soapy water and rinse in boiling water.
Place in a large saucepan and then cover with
hot water. With the lid on, bring the water to the
boil and continue boiling for 15 minutes. Turn off
the heat, then leave the jars in the hot water until
just before they are to be filled. Invert the jars
onto clean kitchen paper to dry. Sterilize the lids
for 5 minutes, by boiling, or according to the
manufacturer's instructions. Jars should be filled
and sealed while they are still hot.

contents

Why Trees Can't Dance and Chillies Rock

It's amazing what you can achieve when you live too far from anyone to hear them telling you that it won't work.

In the spring of 2005, I began growing chillies on a beautiful if unlikely site clinging to the very edge of the North Pennines in northern England. Sixty types of chilli from every corner of the world were planted with a happy optimism that seemed to fly in the face of conventional horticultural wisdom. At 600 feet above sea level, the project was seen as a challenge. Despite many, many mistakes, by the late summer we had our first, staggeringly large, crop of chillies.

They may have come from the tropics of the world but they seemed happier to be here than we had ever imagined, and I soon found myself running the world's most northerly chilli farm. I had never intended to become a farmer or even a horticulturalist but, despite myself, by this time I suppose I had. My simple intention was to plant and grow chillies to get top-quality, fresh ingredients to make some of the dishes I had enjoyed on my travels. The reality was slightly different; I had polytunnels full of plants that needed constant attention and come the summer, I had mountains of fresh chillies and no sensible idea of what to do with most of them. I already had a full-time business to run as a landscape photographer and I really didn't need another one.

However, you can never escape your upbringing and I could just hear my dad saying, 'if something is worth doing at all, it is worth doing properly', so with a great deal of help, a disused stable was converted into a small commercial kitchen and we began the exhaustive process of taking the traditional chilli recipes I had gathered and turning them into what we hoped would become the world's best culinary chilli sauces! We began selling at farmers' markets and, as our confidence grew, through delis and farm stores, eventually taking them to national trade shows and developing a network of outlets selling our range throughout the UK and Europe.

Six years on and every day is still devoted to meeting our own ludicrously high standards for the chilli sauces, marinades and ever-growing list of chilli condiments we produce. All our sauces are still lovingly made by hand to our (daftly) exacting specifications. We are lucky to have considerably more comfortable premises (although still a little chilly in the winter) and a small and devoted team who are tireless in their pursuit of chilli excellence. We now supply everyone from independent stores and local delis through to major multiple retailers both in the UK and abroad. But none of this has ever compromised our own belief that quality matters; each recipe is the product of many hours of hard labour over a hot stove with the finest natural ingredients, and we know that you (and your taste buds) appreciate that!

We often get asked why we call ourselves Trees Can't Dance. Trees have an interesting place in folklore throughout the world. The idea of a dreaming tree, somewhere of permanence to go and sit, think and solve your problems is a common theme not only in Celtic tradition but also in the cultures of Native American Indians, from which most modern chilli plants originated.

You may not be able to solve all your problems by thinking about them, but combine it with dancing and who knows?

The History and Spread of Chillies around the World

Chilli peppers are thought to have originated in the northern Amazon basin and so, by natural geographic spread, are indigenous throughout Central America, South America, the West Indies and the most southerly states of the USA.

The Tepin or Chiltepin pepper (*Capsicum annuum var. glabriusculum*) is reputed to be the oldest variety in the world and is commonly called the 'Mother chilli'. It grows wild in northern Mexico and up into Arizona and Texas where it is now the State chilli. It is particularly hard to domesticate but in the wild it grows best in seemingly impossibly harsh habitats. In areas of extremely low rainfall, such as the Sonoran desert, it can be found thriving in the partial shade provided by a Desert Oak or Mesquite. In these conditions this supposedly annual plant has been known not only to survive but also to fruit for up to 20 years. This is an interesting feature of most chillies; if they are in conditions they like, they will not only thrive for several years, they will also be more prolific fruiters in their second, third and fourth years.

The Tepin is truly a wild pepper and it is further south in Peru and Bolivia where we find possibly the earliest domestication of a variety of chilli, Rocoto or Locoto, some 5,000–6,000 years ago. Evidence has also been found for chilli cultivation in Ecuador from around the same period. Later, the Aztecs were famous for their love of chilli and it featured heavily in their diet. The favourite drink of the Aztec emperors was a combination of chilli and chocolate. Such is their connection with these peppers that the word 'chilli' is derived directly from an Aztec or Nahuatl word; as is 'chocolate' for that matter!

The Portuguese traders of the sixteenth century were behind the spread of chillies around the world. At the time, the Portuguese empire, the first truly global empire, traded with and often colonized areas as widespread as South America, East and West Africa, China, India and Japan. In 1500, the explorer Cabral landed (probably by accident) in Brazil and over the next 200 years, chillies spread quite swiftly through the Empire, eventually becoming indigenous to the cuisine of all the Portuguese colonies.

Although as early as the sixteenth century the monks of Spain and Portugal experimented widely with chillies in cooking, quite strangely the use of chilli peppers did not spread widely across Europe from Portugal but rather back from India along the spice routes through central Asia and Turkey. The British colonization of India marks the beginning of the spread of chilli and in particular curry spices into British cuisine. Initially this was in the form of fish molee and lamb curry, staple dishes of the Raj.

Today, an astonishing 7 million tonnes of chillies are grown every year worldwide. Although Mexico still grows the widest variety, India is the largest producer, growing approximately 1.1 million tonnes and supplying nearly 25% of the world export market for red chillies. China is the second largest producer and is likely to overtake India in the next few years.

Folklore and Unusual Uses

Throughout the world and all through history, chillies have been put to various exotic and unusual uses – from deterring vampires and werewolves in Eastern Europe, to deterring marauding wild elephants in modern-day Assam. They are used in a significant proportion of the most celebrated hangover cures worldwide and can even be an active ingredient in make up – as blusher, giving cheeks a healthy glow. Chilli eye drops have been used as a cure for headaches and chilli powder has even been rubbed on the thumbs and fingernails of children to prevent them sucking their thumbs and biting their nails.

Health and Dietary Benefits

Chillies are cholesterol free, low sodium, low calorie, rich in vitamins A and C, and a good source of folic acid, potassium and vitamin E. They have a long history as a traditional remedy for, amongst others, anorexia and vertigo. They have more scientifically recognized application in the treatment of asthma, arthritis, blood clots, cluster headaches, postherpetic neuralgia (shingles) and burns.

By weight, green chillies contain about twice the amount of vitamin C found in citrus fruits. Red chillies contain more vitamin A than carrots. To put this into context, eating 100 g/3½ oz. fresh green chilli can give up to 240% of an adult's recommended daily allowance of vitamin C.

As I've mentioned, chillies are very low in sodium, containing 3.5–5.7 mg per 100 g/3½ oz., but they are big on flavour. So, adding chilli spice to meals adds seasoning and pungency, counteracting the need for salt and bringing the sodium level down even more. Moreover, chillies contain about 37 calories per 100 g/3½ oz., depending on the variety. Eating meals with approximately 3 g chilli causes the body to burn on average 45 more calories than an equivalent meal that does not contain the additional chilli. After eating, our metabolic rate increases – this is the 'diet-induced thermic effect' – but chillies can boost this effect by up to a factor of 25. So eating meals with chilli can reduce the effective calorific content!

Identifying Chillies

All chillies belong to the Capsicum family, of which there are 5 different species. As most specific varieties have spread around the world, they have been given common names in each geographical area and even naturally crossbred with locally indigenous species. This can make them extremely tricky to identify – taste is perhaps the most effective method, closely followed by our incredibly insightful sense of smell. Each species has common varieties with which it is easy to become familiar while you are perfecting your own individual olfactory and organoleptic identification technique!

Capsicum Annuum, meaning annual, is the most common. This, however, is misleading in itself as all pepper plants, given favourable conditions, are perennial. The *Annuum* species contains most of the more common varieties of chillies, including the Jalapeños, Cayennes, Poblano, Serrano, regular sweet/bell peppers and the 'mother' of all chillies, the infamous Chiltepin.

Capsicum Frutescens tends to have a quite limited variety of pod shapes but still contains some the best-known chilli varieties. The Tabasco chilli made famous in McIlhenny's ubiquitous hot sauce is part of this species, as is the Bird's Eye chilli and most of the common Thai chillies. It also contains perhaps the best-named chilli around – the Malawian Kambuzi.

Capsicum Chinense, or Chinese Capsicum, contains most of the hottest varieties of chillies: Habanero, Scotch Bonnet, Datil and even the super-hot Naga varieties, although it has recently been shown that some of the hottest Nagas in fact share genetic material with the *Capsicum Frutescens* species. These varieties have a very distinctive, fruity aroma and impart that characteristic to any dish prepared with them.

Capsicum Pubescens is a species characterized, as the name suggests, by coming from plants with hairy leaves and stems. They are mostly found in South America and can have significant hardy qualities that allow them to grow at some altitude in Chile and Peru. The most common chilli pepper from this species is the Rocoto or Manzano.

Capsicum Baccatum is another widespread species throughout South America and includes many of the Aji family of chilli peppers prevalent in South American cooking. These varieties are not very common outside their native countries but you occasionally see them grown commercially in southern areas of the USA, where they are frequently referred to as chilenos. The Baccatum plants tend to grow quite tall and tree-like. The peppers themselves are often described as fruity or even citrusy in flavour.

Dan's Simple Guide to Growing Chillies

If you can grow chillies in the wilds of Northumberland, then you can grow them just about anywhere. Like many non-indigenous plants we now enjoy growing in unusual locations, they need a little extra care and protection, particularly in the winter time when temperatures and light levels can be both inconsistent and, to be honest, a little disappointing.

I have fond memories of planting my first trays of chilli seeds in a triple-insulated and heated greenhouse with the wind howling outside and snow piling up on the roof. It was the end of December in northern England and I still remember the thrill of seeing the first shoots appearing through the soil – and the sheer dread of receiving the utilities bill for the cost of heating the greenhouse through the chilliest winter I can remember. You, however, don't need to go this far; if you have a warm windowsill, you can give your plants a great start in life!

You can plant your chilli seeds anytime between end of winter and end of spring, but by planting them early you give the chillies time to ripen in the warm summer months and some will even be ready in time to spice up your summer barbecues. It is worth noting that the hottest (and more unusual) varieties of chilli tend to have the longest growing season as they are used to life in the tropics where temperatures are consistent all year round.

First, fill a multicell seed tray with multipurpose compost, firm down and moisten with water. Place a seed in each cell and lightly cover with compost and water again using a very fine spray so as not to disturb or compress the soil too much. I often cover my freshly sown seeds in a thin layer of vermiculite rather than compost – this has a more open structure and makes it easier for the fragile first shoots of growth to push up into the light. It also acts as a layer of insulation, helping the compost to retain warmth.

If you live in a relatively cool climate, it won't be possible to start growing the chillies outside. In this case, if your seed tray did not come with a clear lid then improvise by placing clingfilm/plastic wrap over the tray to create a greenhouse effect and place in an airing cupboard or anywhere similarly warm to germinate. Chilli seeds like temperatures of around 25°C/77°F to encourage relatively swift germination. At too low a temperature, germination can become sporadic and take far longer than expected.

Check your seeds daily for signs of life and keep the compost moist. Be careful not to overwater them; the compost should be slightly damp to the touch but not sodden or too wet.

As soon as seedlings appear (this can take 2–4 weeks), they need sunlight, so put them somewhere warm with plenty of daylight – a windowsill above a radiator is ideal. Keep the compost moist; at this point it is ideal to water from below by placing the multicell tray in a secondary seed tray lined with capillary matting, which is also easier to keep damp. The moisture will be drawn up into the compost and will in turn encourage the plants to put down strong roots to reach the moisture. Feel the surface of the compost daily to check that it is sufficiently moist. Remember that young seedlings are very fragile and can be scorched if left in direct sunlight, particularly as the heat from the sun increases in the springtime.

When the seedlings sprout a second set of leaves (their first true leaves), transplant them to their own pots – a 7-cm/3-inch diameter pot is good. Pop out your seedlings from the tray, being careful not to damage the roots. Fill the pot with compost, moisten with a little water and dig a well for the seedling. Drop it in and gently firm the compost around it.

You can boost your crop by feeding your plants once a week with diluted liquid tomato fertilizer.

Once your plants reach between 12 and 15 cm/ 5 and 6 inches, it's time to move them to a bigger pot. A 12-cm/5-inch diameter will be big enough for one plant or you can fit 3 in a 30-cm/12-inch pot. Fill the pot with compost to about 1 cm/⅓ inch from the top. Don't worry if you cover up some of the stem, as the plants will sprout new roots from the buried area.

By the time your plants are about 20 cm/8 inches tall, it's a good idea to give them some support by gently tying them to a bit of cane with some twine. As they grow, this can also be used to tie supports for the fruit-laden branches, as they can become too heavy to support themselves.

When they reach 30 cm/12 inches, pinch out the growing tips to encourage outward 'bushy' growth. This is ideally done just above the fifth set of leaves.

By end of spring (depending on where you are in the country), it's warm enough to put your plants outside. Make sure they are in a sheltered area but where they'll receive plenty of sunlight – ideally against a wall facing the sun so that the latent heat built up in the wall will keep them warmer if nighttime temperatures drop a little low. If you're

growing tropical varieties, ie Habaneros, or live somewhere particularly cold, it is far better to grow them in a greenhouse if you have one, or even on a warm windowsill.

At this stage, it might be an idea to move your plants to a bigger, sturdier pot; a 20-cm/8-inch diameter is big enough for each plant. Keep a daily eye on your plants for signs of aphids; chilli plants, like tomatoes, are a favourite of greenfly and whitefly. If you do find a few on your plant, remove them by hand or with an application of soft soap solution.

Continue feeding your plant with the fertilizer dilution (as you would a tomato plant), as per the manufacturer's recommendations. Also be sure to check that the compost is moist. By now the plant should be flowering; it's these flowers which, when pollinated by insects and bees, will develop into chillies. You can help the plants out by doing some hand pollination! This means dabbing a cotton bud into each flower in turn thus mimicking the way a bee may move the pollen from flower to flower. Doing this will greatly increase your fruit yield!

You should be able to harvest some of your chillies six months after you first sowed the seeds, however varieties such as the Habanero take longer to develop. It's a good idea to harvest the first green chillies early, as chilli plants will fruit a few times across the season (spring to autumn) and harvesting will encourage a bigger second growth. Simply snip the chilli pods at the stalk. Once you've done this, you can let the next fruit mature to red for a more rounded flavour.

Although we view chillies as annual plants in the UK, their fruit yields will increase in the second and third years if you can successfully 'over-winter' them. To do this, at the end of the growing season, choose a healthy plant and cleanly cut it back to leave the stem and a few strong healthy branches. Make sure that the plant is free from pests and that the compost is quite fresh. Place the plant on a warm windowsill, trying to avoid cold drafts, and give an occasional modest feed of diluted liquid tomato fertilizer to help boost the plant's 'immune system'. A successfully over-wintered plant will begin to produce growth and in turn, fruit earlier and more prolifically than a plant grown from seed that year. Eventually, after about four to five years, yields begin to fall and it's time to retire that plant!

Now all that's left is to transform your chillies into delicious dinners, sauces, marinades and preserves.

Where Does the Heat Come from?

The heat in chillies comes predominantly from a natural alkaloid chemical compound called capsaicin. When we eat a chilli, the presence of this compound will immediately be sensed by the pain receptors located in your mouth and nose, and eventually your stomach. These cells send a message to the brain to release endorphins into the body. The rush of these natural painkillers often produces a feeling of great wellbeing and it is this sensation that frequent consumers of hot chillies can become addicted to. Like all addictions though, in order to maintain the intensity of this reaction, it becomes necessary to consistently increase the dose! In 2006, it was discovered that tarantula venom activates the same pathway of pain as capsaicin. Not only is this the first demonstration of a shared pathway in both plant and animal 'anti-mammal' defence, but it also gives a clear indication of how potent capsaicin can be.

If you have ever been tempted to take a bite of even a fairly mild chilli, you will know the burning sensation that capsaicin produces – and we have all seen how competitive eating chillies can get! So what are the remedies if the burning gets too much?

Firstly, the things to avoid are water or water-based drinks – this includes beer. In many cases they will actually make the sensation more intense. Capsaicin is not soluble in water and although alcohol is a solvent to capsaicin, it is not a neutralizer, so it is likely that relief will only be temporary and may well carry the burn to other areas of the mouth and throat. It is widely accepted that the most effective remedy is to take a small mouthful of vegetable oil and swill this around your mouth. Due to the hydrophobic composition of capsaicin (like that of oil), it will form a solution with the oil. Spit the oil out and it will take a significant amount of the 'heat' with it. Other effective remedies

are drinking cold milk, yogurt or a cool sugar syrup solution. These methods work equally well if you find yourself with a bad case of Hunan hand, which occurs when skin burns due to overexposure to chillies. Although not common in the UK, overexposure to chilli peppers is one of the most common plant-related symptoms presented at hospital emergency and poison centres throughout regions where peppers are grown and processed on a large scale.

The heat in chillies is thought to be their natural defence against mammals who, when eating them, would crush their seeds with their molars; thus preventing the plants reseeding. This is further supported by the fact that birds, who pass the seeds directly through their digestive systems, are unaffected by the capsaicin that gives chillies their heat; thus allowing the plants, via birds, to spread their coverage more widely than relying on the natural distribution of the wind and the mammals who happened to swallow the fruit whole.

Contrary to popular belief, the seeds of the fruit are not the source of the chilli's heat. The hottest part of the chilli is in fact the placenta that holds the seeds to the internal walls of the fruit. Its heat is in turn due to its direct contact with the tiny glands that actually produce the capsaicin within the wall of the chilli. It is also worth noting that the precise make up of the different capsaicinoids within various chilli varieties can actually deliver the sensation of 'heat' in different ways for different people.

This illustrates one of the key problems facing Wilbur Lincoln Scoville when in 1912 he created his now legendary 'Scoville Organoleptic Test'. This was the first attempt to devise an accurate way of gauging the hotness of chilli peppers. A panel of (usually) five volunteers tasted extracts from specific chillies added in exact quantities to a sugar and water solution. The first point at which the chilli heat was undetectable gave the Scoville rating for that chilli. For example, if a Naga Jolokia was rated at 1,000,000 Scovilles, its extract would need to be diluted over 1,000,000 times before the heat became undetectable to the taster. It relied greatly for its consistency on the taste buds of the volunteers. Thus, although it provided interesting comparisons between varieties of chillies, it was too subjective for reliable results.

Currently, 'heat' is measured using high-performance liquid chromatography (HPLC). In its simplest form, this separates the capsaicinoids from all other liquids present in the chilli. This allows the concentration of heat-giving compounds to be calculated in parts per million. The unit of measurement in this case is not the Scoville, but the American Spice Trade Association pungency unit, or ASTA for short. Despite the consistency of test results within any particular lab using this method, it is interesting to note that results produced by different labs relating to a single variety of chilli can show wide variances in the final heat levels recorded. This illustrates the difficulties in accurately assessing the heat of an overall chilli cultivar rather than a single pod. At its most basic, heat levels in a single species of chilli can vary by anything up to a factor of 10; so you may get a very hot one or a not so hot one. The heat can also be heavily influenced by external factors, such as soil, temperature, humidity and feed regime, as well as the genetic make up of the original plant from which the seed was gathered.

To get from the ASTA unit to the approximate Scoville rating for a chilli we need to multiply by 15; however, as has been illustrated, the results should be seen as indications of heat rather than fact.

It is generally accepted that pure capsaicin has a Scoville rating of around 16,000,000. However this is not the hottest alkaloid found in the natural world. Resiniferatoxin that exists in the sap of some Euphorbias (which grow wild in Morocco) is 1,000 times hotter that pure capsaicin, giving it a Scoville rating of 16,000,000,000!

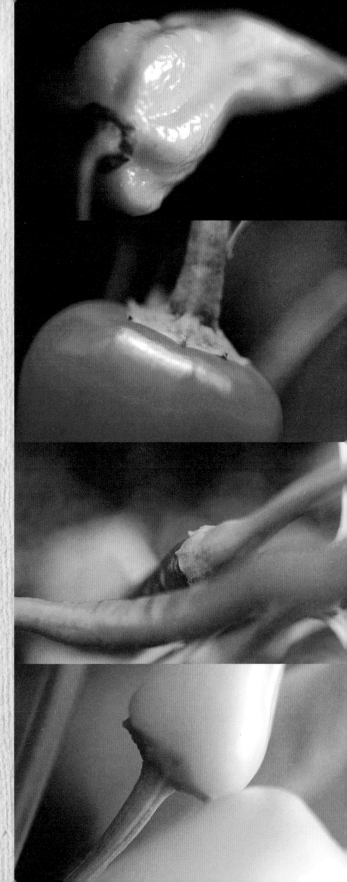

soups & salads

Hot Vegetable Chowder

Chilli Billi Bi, or Cream of Mussel Soup

Spanish Potato, Garlic & Chorizo Soup

Butternut Squash & Coconut Milk Soup

Thai Beef Noodle Soup

Trini Saltfish Buljol

Thai-spiced Rare Beef & Warm Rice Noodle Salad

Beef Carpaccio with Green Salad
& Horseradish Dressing

))))) Hot Chilli Vegetable Chowder

This chowder is a vegetarian dish but is in no way a mild, delicate option. It can be an extremely hot and robust dish indeed. It has a good number of chillies and they impart a tremendous flavour but I would suggest making it with mostly mild and medium chillies unless you like things really spicy.

2 tablespoons olive oil

1 large onion, finely chopped

100 g/3–4 oz. mixed chillies (mild, medium or hot), deseeded and finely chopped, plus extra to garnish

3 celery sticks, chopped

2 potatoes (about 225 g/7 oz.), scrubbed and diced

7-cm/2¾-in. piece of fresh ginger, peeled and grated into a bowl to retain the juice (ie about 2½–3 teaspoons grated ginger)

1 small courgette/zucchini, chopped

1 fresh bay leaf

sprig of fresh thyme

600 ml/2½ cups hot vegetable stock

2 corn cobs/ears of corn

300 ml/1¼ cups milk

300 g/10 oz. green beans, sliced into 1.5-cm/¾-inch pieces

bunch of fresh flat leaf parsley, finely chopped

sea salt and freshly ground white pepper

12 fresh basil leaves, torn, to serve

small bunch of fresh chives, snipped, to serve

Serves 6

Heat the oil in a large saucepan over medium heat and gently fry the onion for 1 minute. Add the chillies, celery, potatoes, ginger and courgette/zucchini, then fry for a further 2–3 minutes.

Add the bay leaf, thyme, ¼ teaspoon white pepper and hot stock and gently bring to the boil. Reduce the temperature and simmer for about 15 minutes, or until the potatoes are cooked.

Meanwhile, put the corn upright on a board and strip the kernels by running a sharp knife carefully downward. Set the kernels aside.

Remove the pan from the heat, discard the bay leaf and thyme sprig and purée the soup with a hand blender until smooth. Alternatively, let cool for a few minutes, then transfer to a blender and pulse until smooth. Return the soup to the pan.

Stir in the milk, then add the beans and reserved corn kernels. Mix thoroughly and simmer for about 12–15 minutes until the beans and corn are tender. Add the parsley and season to taste with salt and white pepper.

Divide the chowder between 6 warm bowls and garnish with the fresh basil, chives and a little more of the chopped chillies.

MY TIP: For a seafood twist, add 250 g/8 oz. cooked/lump white crabmeat about 5 minutes before the end of cooking. Mix thoroughly before serving.

> **RECOMMENDED CHILLIES:** Nu Mex Red, Santa Fe, Guajillo, Jalapeño, Serrano, Cheyenne.

Chilli Billi Bi, or Cream of Mussel Soup

The sustainability of mussel farming in Maine and on the UK's coastline, and the low impact it has on our marine environment make using more of this sort of seafood in our everyday dishes simple common sense. This is a slightly modern take on the classic Breton dish. It is supposedly named after William B. Leeds (Billy B) who reputedly ate it so often at Maxim's in Paris that the owner changed its name in his honour!

1.5–2 kg/3½–4½ lbs. fresh mussels, in their shells

75 g/5 tablespoons butter

1 tablespoon olive oil

2 shallots, chopped

2 garlic cloves, crushed

2 celery sticks, chopped

1 hot red chilli, deseeded and finely chopped

1 fresh bay leaf

250 ml/1 cup dry white wine

small pinch of saffron strands, crushed

600 ml/2½ cups fish stock

2 tablespoons plain/all-purpose flour

200 ml/¾ cup double/heavy cream

ground Cayenne pepper, to dust

2 tablespoons snipped fresh chives, to serve

1 tablespoon chopped fresh curly parsley, to serve

sea salt and freshly ground black pepper

very large stockpot with a lid

muslin/cheesecloth

triturator (optional)

Serves 4

RECOMMENDED CHILLIES:
Bird's Eye or Thai Hot.

Prepare the mussels by removing the beards (the seaweed-like stringy threads protruding from the shells), then rinsing the mussels well in cold water. Discard any that are broken or gape and fail to close during handling or when tapped sharply.

Heat 25 g/1½ tablespoons of the butter and the oil in the very large stockpot over medium heat and fry the shallots for a few moments until softened but not brown. Add the garlic, celery, chilli, bay leaf and white wine. Cover with a lid and bring to the boil. Add the mussels and cook, covered, for 2–5 minutes, shaking the pan occasionally, until all the mussels have opened. Put a double layer of muslin/cheesecloth into a second large pan and strain the cooking liquor from the mussels into it. Tip the mussels into a large bowl.

Add the saffron to the strained cooking liquor and infuse for a few moments before adding the fish stock. Return to the heat and allow to gently warm. Set aside until required.

Remove the meat from the mussel shells, discarding any that have not opened. Put two-thirds of the mussel meat in a food processor and pulse until blended to a coarse purée. If liquid is required to aid this process, add a little of the reserved cooking liquor. Place this purée into a triturator, stiff, coarse sieve/strainer or fine colander and with the back of a spoon, press as much of the mixture as you can through the mesh back into a clean bowl – it is important to get as through as possible, as this will really benefit the final soup. Discard what's left in the sieve/strainer. This process may need to be done in batches.

In a third pan, heat the butter over low heat until it melts. Add the flour to make a roux and gently heat, stirring constantly for 3–5 minutes. Whisk the reserved cooking liquor into the roux. Bring to the boil, stirring well, then reduce the heat and simmer gently for about 20 minutes. Add the smooth mussel mixture and gently mix through. Whisk in the cream and finally add the reserved whole mussels. Reheat without bringing to the boil. Season to taste with salt and pepper. Divide the soup between 4 warm bowls and garnish with a dusting of Cayenne pepper and the fresh chives and parsley.

)))) Spanish Potato, Garlic & Chorizo Soup

This is a marvellously rustic and enjoyable soup to both make and eat. The chorizo sausage adds a lovely warm background flavour to the dish and the toasted almonds put a delicate sweet crunch into every mouthful. Serve it with the best, freshest bread.

3 tablespoons olive oil, plus extra to drizzle

250 g/8 oz. chorizo sausage, sliced into 1.5-cm/¾-inch pieces

1 large onion, chopped

4 large garlic cloves, thinly sliced

1 hot red chilli, deseeded and finely chopped

125 ml/½ cup white wine

1 kg/2¼ lbs. potatoes, peeled and cut into 2.5-cm/1-inch cubes

500 ml/2 cups hot chicken or vegetable stock

1 tablespoon sweet smoked paprika (pimentón dulce)

½–1 teaspoon celery salt

1 teaspoon dried tarragon

sea salt and freshly ground black pepper

50 g/⅓ cup blanched almonds, toasted and coarsely ground with a pestle and mortar, to garnish

chopped fresh flat leaf parsley, to garnish

Serves 4–5

Heat the oil in a heavy-based saucepan over medium heat and fry the chorizo for 2 minutes. Reduce the heat and add the onion, garlic and chilli. Fry gently for 10 minutes, or until the onion has softened.

Pour the white wine into the pan and gently simmer for another minute to evaporate the alcohol. Add the potatoes and stock and mix well. Add the paprika, celery salt and tarragon, stir thoroughly and bring back to the boil.

Reduce the heat to low and gently simmer until the potatoes are cooked. Add a little boiling water to the pan if it looks like there's not enough liquid. Season with salt and pepper to taste.

Garnish with a scattering of the almonds, a little parsley and a fine drizzle of olive oil.

MY TIP: I recommend that you use sweet smoked paprika (Spanish pimentón dulce) for this recipe, but stick to the unsmoked, sweet variety if you don't like smoky flavours.

RECOMMENDED CHILLIES: Guindilla or any hot Cayenne variety.

))) Butternut Squash & Coconut Milk Soup

To say a soup is warming is perhaps stating the obvious, but this one is supremely satisfying. Not only does it taste fantastic, combining hints of the East with all the best bits of a crisp autumn day, but the colour is superb. In our household this forms a staple part of our winter diet, and we often have a huge pan of it on the go for get-togethers during the colder months.

1 butternut squash, peeled, deseeded and cut into 2-cm/1-inch cubes

1 sweet potato, peeled and cut into 2-cm/1-inch cubes

3 garlic cloves, bruised and skin on

4 tablespoons olive oil

1 onion, finely chopped

1 celery stick, finely chopped

2 teaspoons vegetable bouillon powder

1 medium–hot red chilli, deseeded and finely chopped

2.5-cm/1-inch piece of fresh ginger, peeled and grated

400-ml/14-oz. can of coconut milk

sea salt and freshly ground black pepper

chopped fresh coriander/cilantro, to garnish

toasted sesame oil, to drizzle

Serves 4–6

RECOMMENDED CHILLIES: Any medium–hot Thai-style chilli, Kung Pao or small supermarket hot red.

Preheat the oven to 180°C (350°F) Gas 4.

Put the butternut squash, sweet potato and garlic into a roasting dish, drizzle half the olive oil over the top, cover loosely with foil and roast in the preheated oven for about 40 minutes, or until the squash, potato and garlic are soft.

Meanwhile, heat the remaining olive oil in a saucepan over low heat and gently fry the onion and celery for about 10 minutes, or until soft. Add the bouillon powder, chilli and ginger – it will help if you add a couple of tablespoons of water at this point to stop the bouillon from sticking to the bottom of the pan.

Once the squash and potato are cooked, add them together with their cooking juices to the pan with the onion mixture, and give everything a good stir. If the garlic is soft enough, squeeze this out of the skins and into the pan too, but don't worry if they have become too crispy – just discard them, as the squash and potato will have taken on a deliciously subtle garlicky flavour while roasting.

Now add the coconut milk to the pan and allow to simmer very gently for a couple of minutes, uncovered. Remove the pan from the heat and purée the soup with a hand blender until smooth. Alternatively, let cool for a few minutes, then transfer to a blender and blend until smooth. If the soup is too thick, feel free to add some hot water to loosen it slightly. Season to taste with salt and pepper.

Garnish with a little coriander/cilantro and a drizzle of sesame oil.

)))) Thai Beef Noodle Soup

This recipe came from Jamie Cottell, a great friend of mine and also a rather wonderful chef. He is not given to over-excitement about recipes in general but this is a bit special and the result of many hours over a hot stove! It came with very specific, tongue-in-cheek instructions: "...do not show this recipe to anyone from Thailand as I fear they may blush somewhat with embarrassment; THIS IS HOW YOU DO IT!"

4 tablespoons toasted cashews

Broth base

1 lemongrass stick
700 ml/3 cups cold beef stock
2 tablespoons soy sauce
2 tablespoons nam pla fish
   sauce
2 tablespoons palm sugar
grated zest and freshly
   squeezed juice of 1 lime
400-ml/14-oz. can of coconut
   milk

Soup bits & pieces

200 g/7 oz. thin rice noodles
2 teaspoons toasted sesame
   oil, plus extra to drizzle
2 eggs, lightly beaten
2 garlic cloves, crushed
5-cm/2-inch piece of fresh
   galangal (or ginger), grated
2 small red chillies, deseeded
   and thinly sliced, plus extra
   to garnish
2 kaffir lime leaves
2 big handfuls of spinach
   leaves
4 chestnut mushrooms, sliced
2 tablespoons chopped fresh
   coriander/cilantro, plus
   extra leaves to garnish
5 tablespoons julienned carrot
4 Baby Gem lettuce leaves,
   thinly sliced
1 shallot, julienned
40 g/½ cup bean sprouts
280 g/10 oz. sirloin steak,
   sliced as thinly as you can

Serves 2 as a main or 4 as a starter

To make the broth base, bash the lemongrass carefully with the handle of a knife to bruise it. Place it with all the other broth base ingredients in a saucepan, bring to a simmer and taste! Add more seasoning if required and discard the lemongrass.

For the soup bits & pieces, blanch the noodles in a pan of boiling water for 5 minutes or until cooked, and refresh under cold water.

Put the toasted sesame oil in a non-stick frying pan and heat. Pour the beaten eggs into the hot pan and fry gently, allowing no colour to develop and without stirring. You will eventually get a sort of egg pancake. Let cool slightly to handle, then transfer it to a board and slice it into 3-mm/⅛-inch strips. Divide the pieces of egg between 2 or 4 soup bowls (depending on whether you are making 2 mains or 4 starters).

Divide all the remaining ingredients that make up the soup bits & pieces between the bowls, along with the blanched noodles. Bring the broth base back to a simmer, then pour it into the soup bowls – the hot broth will reheat and/or cook all the ingredients. Garnish each bowl with whole coriander/cilantro leaves, a few slices of chilli, a drizzle of sesame oil and the toasted cashew nuts.

MY TIP: Mai Fun noodles are a good choice here but if they are not available in your local Asian store, there will definitely be a close rice-noodle substitute available which will work fine in this recipe.

> **RECOMMENDED CHILLIES: Thai Hot or Bird's Eye.**

))))) Trini Saltfish Buljol

A very hot breakfast or brunch, this is a great introduction to Caribbean food and to the many and varied ways of using salt cod (saltfish to West Indians and bacalao to Spaniards!) It always looks like such an unpromising ingredient but you can't help but become a fan when it helps deliver flavours like these. I would consider the perfect place to serve this to be a wedding breakfast – where you think everyone just needs pepping up a bit! It's also great on toast on a Sunday morning.

225 g/7 oz. salt cod (bacalao)
200 ml/¾ cup milk
1 fresh bay leaf
1 slice of lemon
25 g/2 tablespoons butter
5–6 mixed peppercorns
1 teaspoon Dijon mustard
1 large onion, very finely chopped
1 large tomato, diced
1 ripe pointed red sweet/bell pepper, deseeded and diced (or ordinary red sweet/bell pepper)
1 Trinidad Congo chilli, deseeded and finely chopped
1 Hungarian Hot Wax chilli, deseeded and finely chopped
½ teaspoon freshly ground black pepper
3 tablespoons olive oil
a few Romaine lettuce leaves
2 hard-boiled eggs, sliced
1 avocado, sliced

Serves 2–4

You will need to start preparing the salad the day before you serve it. Put the salt cod in a bowl, cover with cold water and let soak for 24 hours in the fridge, changing the water frequently.

The next day, drain the soaked cod and pat dry with kitchen paper/paper towels. Put the cod in a large frying pan and add the milk, bay leaf, lemon, butter and peppercorns. Cover with a lid and poach gently for 20 minutes, or until the fish is soft. Remove from the poaching liquor (reserving the liquor) and let cool. Debone and flake the fish into a bowl.

Return the pan of poaching liquor to a medium heat and cook, stirring regularly to prevent a skin forming. Once the liquid has reduced by half, remove the bay leaf, lemon and peppercorns and discard. Remove from the heat and stir in the mustard. Let cool for a while, until thickened.

To the flaked fish, add the onion, tomato and sweet/bell pepper, chillies, black pepper and olive oil and mix well. Serve on the lettuce leaves and garnish with the eggs and avocado. Serve with the thickened milk/mustard combination in a small bowl.

MY TIP: Trinidad Congo chillies are members of the Habanero family of chillies. They are renowned for their pungency and wonderful fruity flavour and aroma. If you can't get hold of these, any Habanero/Scotch Bonnet variety of chilli will work perfectly in this recipe. Hungarian Hot Wax chillies are mild peppers that add a delicious crunch and a modest kick to any salad. If these are not available, substitute with half a yellow sweet/bell pepper.

> **RECOMMENDED CHILLIES:** Trinidad Congo, Antillais Caribbean, Scotch Bonnet, Hungarian Hot Wax, Santa Fe.

Thai-spiced Rare Beef & Warm Rice Noodle Salad

One of the most enjoyable elements of drifting from a relatively solitary profession like photography to food has been the extraordinary social whirlwind that it seems to create. I have been fortunate to become friends with many astonishingly talented and generous folk over the past years and probably none more so than Owen Potts, who is the source of this recipe. Despite surrounding himself with perpetual frenetic activity, Owen is never too busy for a chat or a beer; or even to drive 300 miles to help spit-roast a pig...but that's another story. This recipe makes a deliciously different and tasty oriental variation on a simple salad.

400 g/14 oz. fillet steak/beef tenderloin

1 tablespoon sunflower oil

100 g/3½ oz. bamboo shoots, finely shredded

100 g/⅔ cup roasted salted peanuts, coarsely ground

200 g/6½ oz. baby spinach leaves

500 g/1 lb. thin rice noodles

1 teaspoon toasted sesame oil

8 spring onions/scallions, thinly sliced

3 tablespoons Nuoc Cham (see page 133)

2 handfuls of fresh coriander/cilantro, finely chopped

2–3 baby courgettes/zucchini (about 200 g/6½ oz.), sliced into ribbons with a mandolin or potato slicer

freshly squeezed juice of ½ lime

a pinch of salt

2 thin red chillies, very thinly sliced

Marinade

1 lemongrass stick, very finely chopped

2 teaspoons Thai red curry paste

2 teaspoons nam pla fish sauce

freshly squeezed juice of ½ lime

Serves 4

To make the marinade, mix the lemongrass, curry paste, fish sauce and lime juice, then place the beef in a shallow dish and cover with the marinade. Cover and refrigerate for as long as possible (30 minutes is OK; overnight would be superb).

Heat the oil in a frying pan over medium heat and fry the marinated beef (reserving any remaining marinade) for 2 minutes each side. Remove from the pan, cover and set aside. In the same pan, quickly fry the bamboo shoots and peanuts with any remaining marinade. Add the spinach to the pan, immediately remove from the heat and cover with a lid to allow the spinach to wilt in the residual heat.

Blanch the noodles in a pan of boiling water for 5 minutes or until cooked. Drain and toss in the sesame oil, spring onions/scallions, Nuoc Cham and half the coriander/cilantro. Meanwhile, thinly slice the beef and keep warm.

Dress the courgettes/zucchini with the lime juice, the remaining coriander/cilantro and the salt.

To assemble, divide the noodles between 4 warm plates, then pile the remaining ingredients on top. Garnish with the sliced chillies.

MY TIP: This recipe would also work extremely well with skinless chicken breast. Unlike the beef which can be served rare, it is important to ensure that the chicken is thoroughly cooked through before serving.

RECOMMENDED CHILLIES: Thai Hot or Bird's Eye.

Beef Carpaccio with Green Salad & Horseradish Dressing

Whether carpaccio really started at Harry's Bar in Venice or not is a point of some contention. There does, however, seem to be little doubt that it was named after the fifteenth-century Italian painter of the same name. It is now generally used to describe any dish of very thinly sliced raw meat or fish. This beautifully flavoured dish makes a very sophisticated lunch for two.

9 tablespoons extra virgin olive oil

sea salt and freshly ground black pepper

Carpaccio

1 tablespoon coriander seeds

1 tablespoon fennel seeds

1 tablespoon cumin seeds

½ teaspoon sweet smoked paprika (pimentón dulce)

½ teaspoon chilli powder, eg ground Ancho or other ground red pepper

2 x 120-g/4-oz. organic (28-day hung) beef fillets/filets mignons, fully trimmed

1 tablespoon sunflower oil

Horseradish dressing

2-cm/1-inch piece of fresh horseradish, finely grated

50 g/3 tablespoons full-fat crème fraîche or sour cream

freshly squeezed juice of 1 small lemon

Green salad

1 Baby Gem or Baby Romaine lettuce, roughly chopped

small bunch of watercress – a mixture of whole leaves and finely chopped

1 chilli, deseeded and finely chopped

60 g/2 oz. cucumber, sliced into ribbons with a mandoline or potato slicer

squeeze of lemon juice

handful of fresh flat leaf parsley, chopped

Serves 2 as a main or 4 as a starter

To make the carpaccio, toast the spice seeds in a dry frying pan over high heat until they begin to pop. Grind the toasted seeds, paprika and chilli powder with a pestle and mortar.

Season the beef with salt and pepper, then roll in the spice mix, pressing down firmly to ensure that the fillets are well coated. Put the sunflower oil in a frying pan over medium heat and sear the fillets until all sides are golden brown – about 1 minute each side. Remove from the pan and set aside to cool. When cool, wrap in clingfilm/plastic wrap and refrigerate.

To make the horseradish dressing, combine 3 tablespoons of the olive oil with all the dressing ingredients and mix well. Season with salt and black pepper. The desired consistency is a little thicker than a normal dressing, but add up to 1 tablespoon water to loosen, if required. Refrigerate until needed.

To make the green salad, mix the lettuce, watercress, chilli and cucumber in a large bowl. In a small bowl, whisk together 5 tablespoons of the olive oil, the lemon juice and parsley and season to taste with salt and pepper. Pour the dressing over the salad and toss well to give an even coating.

Slice the seared beef fillets as thinly as you can, season with more salt and pepper and coat lightly in the remaining olive oil. Arrange the salad on plates, top with the carpaccio and drizzle a little of the horseradish dressing over it.

> **RECOMMENDED CHILLIES:** For the salad, we love ripe, red Cherry Bomb although for a milder alternative Hungarian Hot Wax are ideal. For the chilli powder, pure ground Ancho chilli provides a great balance to the smoky paprika.

nibbles & sharing plates

Mini Crab Cakes with Quick Chilli Lime Mayo

Jalapeño Poppers

Pickled Baby Cucumber

Barbecue Shrimp Marinated in Chilli & Soy

Chilli-marinated Salmon Gravadlax

Chilli Cheese Straws

Tapas of Quick Marinated Olives & Simple Padrón Peppers

Chilli Pickled Onions

)))) Mini Crab Cakes with Quick Chilli Lime Mayo

Nothing represents all that is wonderful and surprising about seafood better than the humble crab. Hidden behind a most unlikely exterior its flavourful, succulent and incredibly versatile meat is a delight. Fresh crab combines wonderfully well with chilli! These mini crab cakes, served with the quickest chilli lime mayo, are great as nibbles with a glass of chilled white wine.

500 g/1 lb. cooked/lump white crabmeat

4 spring onions/scallions, finely chopped

1 garlic clove, crushed

1 hot red or green chilli, deseeded and very finely chopped

1 tablespoon chopped fresh flat leaf parsley or coriander/cilantro

1 tablespoon nam pla (or other) fish sauce

1 teaspoon muscovado/raw cane or light brown sugar

1 egg, beaten

1 teaspoon white wine vinegar

good pinch of sea salt

plain/all-purpose flour, to dust

100 ml/½ cup sunflower or groundnut/peanut oil, for frying

Quick Chilli Lime Mayo (see page 117)

Makes 16

Mix together the crabmeat, spring onions/scallions, garlic, chilli, fresh herbs, fish sauce, sugar, egg, vinegar and salt. This can most easily be done in a food processor; however mixing by hand in a bowl will give more texture to the final crab cakes. Divide into 16 pieces and shape into balls, then flatten to discs. Dust each crab cake lightly with flour and refrigerate for 30 minutes before cooking.

Heat the oil in a large frying pan over medium heat and fry the crab cakes in small batches. Turn frequently and when both sides are golden – about 2 minutes each side – they are ready to serve.

Serve with the quick chilli lime mayo for dipping.

MY TIP: Placing the crab cakes in the fridge for a while before cooking makes them easier to handle and less likely to fall apart during cooking.

RECOMMENDED CHILLIES: Red or green Bird's Eye, Kung Pao or Thai Hot.

))))) Jalapeño Poppers (right)

Jalapeños are ideal for this recipe. They have a juicy flesh that tastes delicious when combined with cheese. If they are not available, I would suggest using red Cherry Bomb chillies which are a little sweeter and often a little hotter too! These poppers will whet your appetite at the start of a barbecue.

20 Jalapeño chillies
140 g/1¼ cups grated mature/sharp cheddar
50 g/⅓ cup plain/all-purpose flour
1 egg, beaten
sunflower oil, for deep frying

cooking thermometer (optional)

Makes 20

Slit the Jalapeños along one side and carefully remove the seeds. Stuff them generously with the grated cheddar.

Put the flour in one shallow bowl and the beaten egg in another. Roll the Jalapeños in the flour, dip in the egg and then coat once more with flour, ensuring that they are completely covered.

Half-fill a large saucepan with oil. Heat until the oil reaches 190°C (375°F) on a cooking thermometer. If you don't have a cooking thermometer, the oil is ready when a 2.5-cm/1-inch cube of white bread dropped into it browns in less than 60 seconds.

Fry the Jalapeños in small batches for 6–7 minutes until golden. Remove with a slotted spoon and drain on kitchen paper/paper towels.

))))) Pickled Baby Cucumber

Although not strictly a chilli recipe, when combined with yogurt or crème fraîche this makes the perfect cooling accompaniment to anything that does contain plenty of chillies. This is the original way that pickles, which later became the universal side order with burgers, were made.

1 fresh bay leaf
½ teaspoon black peppercorns
2 whole cloves
50 g/¼ cup sea salt
100 ml/6 tablespoons cider vinegar
4 garlic cloves, peeled and halved
2 sprigs of fresh tarragon or dill
750 g/1½ lbs. young, small dark-skinned (pickling) cucumbers, topped and tailed

1-kg/quart sealable jar with new lid, sterilized (see page 4)

Makes 1 large jar

Put 600 ml/2½ cups water, the bay leaf, peppercorns, cloves and salt in a small saucepan and bring to the boil. Remove from the heat and let cool.

Add the vinegar and mix. Place 2 of the garlic cloves and one of the herb sprigs in the bottom of the sterilized jar. Pack in the cucumbers, inserting the second sprig of herbs halfway up the jar. Pour in as much of the pickling liquid as required to cover the cucumbers, adding the last of the garlic towards the top of the jar. The jar should be filled to the top with cucumbers and pickling liquid. Tightly seal and invert several times to mix.

Let ferment in a cool, dark place for about 1 month. These pickles should be crunchy and with a slightly sharp taste. Alternatively, speed up the fermentation process by placing the jar on a sunny windowsill for 4–5 days. If you try this route, the pickles should be refrigerated after this period.

)))) Barbecue Shrimp Marinated in Chilli & Soy

Here's a great Asian marinade that is really quick and simple to make and just perfect for prawns/shrimp. Marinating in a bag is also an excellent way to ensure everything gets an even coating of sauce. My favourite aïoli (page 117) is the ideal accompaniment for the spicy prawns/shrimp and juicy tomatoes.

500 g/1 lb. raw tiger prawns/
    jumbo shrimp, peeled but
    tails intact

250 g/8 oz. cherry vine
    tomatoes

4 tablespoons olive oil

1 large green sweet/bell
    pepper, deseeded and cut
    into 3-cm/1¼-inch chunks

2 red Jalapeños, deseeded and
    cut into 1-cm/½-inch pieces

watercress and toasted pita
    bread, to serve

Fresh Aïoli (see page 117),
    to serve

Marinade

1 garlic clove, crushed

1 red chilli, deseeded and
    finely chopped

1 tablespoon sesame oil

2 tablespoons dark soy sauce

grated zest and freshly
    squeezed juice of 1 lime

2 tablespoons dark brown
    sugar

medium sealable plastic food bag

*8 wooden skewers, soaked in
    water overnight*

gas or charcoal barbecue/grill

Serves 4

To make the marinade, mix together all the ingredients and blend to a smooth purée using a hand blender. If you don't have a hand blender, grind to a paste using a pestle and mortar.

Put the prawns/shrimp in the sealable food bag and pour in the marinade. Seal securely. Shake vigorously and when all the prawns/shrimp look well coated, refrigerate, still in the bag, for about 2 hours.

Put the tomatoes and half the olive oil in a small saucepan and gently warm for 5 minutes, or just long enough for the tomatoes to start to soften. Remove from the heat and let cool.

Light your barbecue/grill. Always do this in plenty of time to have built up a good bed of hot ashes or charcoal that have burnt down to a white glow with no visible flames. This normally takes about 45 minutes from lighting.

Take the refrigerated prawns/shrimp out of the bag and place on a plate, reserving any remaining marinade. Thread the marinated prawns/shrimp, tomatoes, sweet/bell pepper and Jalapeños onto the skewers in a repeating sequence and continue until all 8 skewers are filled. Make sure you allow for enough of each ingredient on each skewer, and leave enough space at the ends of the skewers to handle when on the barbecue/grill.

In a small bowl, loosen the reserved marinade with 1–2 tablespoons of the remaining olive oil. Using a pastry brush, liberally coat the skewers with the marinade just before placing on the barbecue/grill.

Cook for a couple of minutes on each side until the prawns/shrimp turn pink and are cooked through. Serve with watercress, toasted pita bread and a good dollop of fresh aïoli.

MY TIP: Be sure to soak the wooden skewers thoroughly, preferably overnight, before making up the skewers for the barbecue. This will prevent them from catching fire while you are cooking!

> **RECOMMENDED CHILLIES:** For the skewers – Jalapeño, Cherry Bomb. For the marinade – Thai-style hot red chilli or red Bird's Eye.

)))) Chilli-marinated Salmon Gravadlax

My brother-in-law Chris made an excellent salmon gravadlax a few years ago for lunch on Boxing Day. At first I was a little sceptical, as I had always felt that curing fish was something of a dark art, but this was delicious and I was inspired to have a go myself. I have always had a fondness for the cured and pickled fish common in Scandinavian cuisine but anticipated it would be as difficult as it looked to achieve tasty results. Happily, despite appearances, it is a surprisingly simple process and there is a great sense of satisfaction from curing and preserving a beautiful piece of fresh fish. This cure also works extremely well with fresh mackerel fillets.

grated zest and freshly
   squeezed juice of 1 lemon

large bunch of fresh dill,
   chopped

brown toast, to serve

very finely grated fresh
   horseradish, to serve

Chilli-infused vodka

75 ml/⅓ cup vodka

1–2 red Bird's Eye chillies,
   chopped

Cure

150 g/⅓ cup sea salt flakes

175 g/a scant cup sugar

3 tablespoons mixed
   peppercorns, freshly and
   coarsely ground

2 small–medium whole
   salmon fillets, skin on and
   pin-boned

*small, sealable jar, for the chilli-
   infused vodka*

*glass or other non-metallic dish
   large enough to hold the
   salmon fillets one on top of
   the other*

*rigid board that will fit inside
   the dish*

Serves 20 as a starter

To make the chilli-infused vodka, pour the vodka into the small jar and add the chopped chillies. Tightly seal and set aside in a warm place for 24 hours. Give the jar a shake whenever you are passing. After this period, strain the infused vodka into a small cup or jar.

To make the cure, mix the salt, sugar and peppercorns in a small bowl. Spread a large sheet of clingfilm/plastic wrap (it will need to be large enough to wrap around the salmon fillets) over the glass or other non-metallic dish large enough to take the salmon fillets. Place one fillet, skin side down, on the clingfilm/plastic wrap. Spread half the cure mixture over the surface of the salmon. Evenly distribute half the lemon zest over the cure, then cover with the dill. Sprinkle the infused vodka over the fillet and cover with the rest of the cure mixture. Place the second fillet, skin side up, on the first fillet.

Wrap the clingfilm/plastic wrap tightly around the salmon. On top of this place the rigid board and weight down with a few heavy cans or jam jars. Refrigerate for 24 hours.

After this period, remove the dish from the fridge, unwrap the fillets and baste with the liquid that has been squeezed from the salmon. Re-wrap, flip over in the dish, weight down and refrigerate for 24 hours.

Remove the salmon from its wrapping, separate the fillets and scrape away any excess cure/lemon/dill mixture. Using a sharp knife, carefully remove the skin. Trim away any brown bits from the skin side of the fillet. Slice very thinly at an oblique angle and serve on brown toast with a dressing of grated horseradish and a dash of lemon juice.

> **RECOMMENDED CHILLIES:** To infuse the vodka quickly, it is good to use a hot chilli such as a red Bird's Eye. There are, however, great subtle variations that you can achieve by incorporating different chilli varieties. Try Aji Limo if you can find them or maybe even a smoked chilli or two.

)))) Chilli Cheese Straws

Here is a brilliantly easy, delicious and impressive nibble to enjoy with a nice cold beer. The pastry is readily available in the chilled or frozen cabinet of any supermarket or convenience store so you don't even need make that. You can also experiment with the filling – some very finely chopped prosciutto or fresh herbs would be tasty additions to this recipe.

500-g/1-lb. pack of puff pastry, thawed if frozen

plain/all-purpose flour, to dust

1 tablespoon Dijon mustard

2 tablespoons milk

1 medium–hot red chilli, deseeded and finely chopped

100 g/¾ cup finely grated Gruyère cheese

1 egg, beaten

2 teaspoons black onion (nigella) seeds

a generous pinch of sea salt

baking sheet, lined with baking parchment

Makes about 16–20

Preheat the oven to 200°C (400°F) Gas 6.

Divide the pastry dough in half. Dust the work surface with flour and roll out the dough into 2 identical sheets approximately 18 cm/ 7 inches wide, 36 cm/ 14 inches long and no more than 3 mm/ ⅛ inch thick.

Mix together the mustard and milk. Brush the mixture over both sheets of dough, then sprinkle the chopped red chilli evenly over just one sheet. Sprinkle the grated cheese evenly on top of the chilli. Now place the second sheet, mustard/milk side down, on top of the cheese and chilli filling and press down firmly, making sure the 2 sheets are well stuck together.

Brush the top of your pastry sandwich with the beaten egg and sprinkle the black onion seeds and sea salt evenly over the sandwich.

With a sharp knife, cut the sandwich into strips about 1–1.5 cm/ ⅜–⅝ inch wide. Carefully twist the strips a couple of times so you get a spiral effect, then lay them on the prepared baking sheet. The straws will spread quite a bit during cooking, so make sure they are well spaced on the baking sheet even if it means that you have to cook them in several batches.

Bake in the preheated oven for 12–15 minutes until the pastry has turned a lovely golden colour and feels crisp at the edges. Allow the straws to firm up for a few minutes on the baking sheet, then transfer carefully to a wire rack to cool slightly before devouring!

MY TIP: Make sure the 2 sheets are firmly pressed together otherwise it will be difficult to twist the pastry without the filling falling out!

> **RECOMMENDED CHILLIES:** Jalapeño or Cheyenne.

Tapas of Quick Marinated Olives & Simple Padrón Peppers

Here are two fun ways to get some chilli in your tapas. The olives can be made well in advance but the Padrón peppers need to be cooked to order. Padrón peppers can sometimes be hard to find, but stock up a little when you do as they keep surprisingly well in the fridge. If you ever find yourself in Barcelona, visit the amazing Santa Caterina food market, designed by the same architects who did the Scottish Parliament building. I seem to recall coming back with nearly 5 kilos/11 pounds of Padrón peppers in my suitcase – well worth the air fare in itself!

Quick marinated olives

200 ml/¾ cup good olive oil

3 garlic cloves, bruised and skin on

large sprig of fresh rosemary

1 hot red chilli, very thinly sliced

grated zest of 1 lemon

400-g/14-oz. can black pitted olives

Simple Padrón peppers

20 pimientos de Padrón (small green fresh Spanish peppers)

1 tablespoon good olive oil

sea salt flakes

Serves 4–6

To make the quick marinated olives, put the oil, garlic and rosemary in a saucepan and heat VERY gently, until the first few bubbles begin to rise up to the surface. Remove the pan from the heat, add the chilli and lemon zest and set aside to cool.

Meanwhile, drain, rinse and pat the olives dry on kitchen paper/paper towels. Place them in a large jam jar or bowl. Once the infused olive oil has cooled, pour it over the drained olives. Leave at room temperature for a minimum of 2 hours before serving, periodically stirring or shaking (if they are in a jam jar!) to allow the flavours to infuse the olives. The longer you can leave them the better the end results will be.

To make the simple Padrón peppers, wash and pat the peppers dry on kitchen paper/paper towels but do not destalk them. Heat the oil in a frying pan over medium heat and fry the peppers in small batches, turning frequently, until they begin to change colour and the skin starts to puff up. Remove from the pan and drain on kitchen paper/paper towels. Season with salt flakes and serve.

Serve your tapas with The Perfect Bloody Mary (page 154) or a glass of ice-cold beer and plenty of bread for mopping up the delicious oil!

MY TIP: Be warned! Although Padrón peppers are generally very mild, about 1 in 10 can have a real hot chilli kick. We occasionally dress the peppers with a little of the oil from the marinated olives, which is delicious!

> **RECOMMENDED CHILLIES:** Padrón peppers are generally available from late June. If you can't find them, mild green chillies can be substituted.

Chilli Pickled Onions

I am lucky enough to work with something of a pickled onion guru. Jamie has been making pickled onions and everything even tangentially related to them for many years, both professionally and domestically. He insists that brining the onions before pickling encourages them to take up more of the flavours infused into the vinegar. He is definitely right! Having tried many different recipes I think these have a great balance of flavour, crunch, sweetness and acidity. Try experimenting with various chillies — adding dried Habaneros works wonderfully well too but does produce wickedly hot onions. It also leaves a rather marvellous vinegar...sprinkle on your fries at your peril!

Brine

125 g/⅔ cup sea salt

1 litre/quart warm water

Pickling Ingredients

500 g/1 lb. pickling onions or small shallots

2 blades of mace

2 dried bay leaves

2 lemongrass sticks

100 ml/6 tablespoons malt vinegar

350 ml/1½ cups white wine (or cider) vinegar

100 g/½ cup (caster) sugar

1 tablespoon sea salt

1 tablespoon coriander seeds

6 red Bird's Eye chillies, halved lengthways and deseeded, or 2 Habanero chillies, quartered lengthways and deseeded

1-litre/quart jar, sterilized (see page 4)

Makes a 1-litre/quart jar

To make the brine, put the salt and warm water in a large bowl and stir to dissolve the salt. Let cool completely.

To prepare the pickling ingredients, top and tail the pickling onions or shallots. Without peeling, place in a large bowl and pour boiling water over them. Leave for about 20 seconds or so to blanch. Replace the water with cold and remove the skins from the onions under the water to prevent any oxidization, which can cause them to get a little tough. Put the skinned onions in the cold brine, cover and let soak for 24 hours.

After 24 hours, refresh the brined onions by rinsing under cold water and quickly drying with kitchen paper/paper towels. Place in the sterilized jar with the mace and bay leaves.

Bash the lemongrass sticks carefully with the handle of a knife to bruise them, then slice lengthways.

Heat the lemongrass, vinegars, 100 ml/⅓ cup water, the sugar, salt and coriander seeds in a stainless steel saucepan. Bring to the boil and simmer for a couple of minutes. Add the chillies and bring back to the boil. Immediately pour the hot contents of the pan over the onions and seal the jar. Invert the jar a couple of times to make sure there is an airtight seal and that no liquid leaks out.

Store in a cool, dark place for as long as you can resist before eating (at least 1 month). Invert the jar regularly during the maturing process.

These little onions are ideally served thinly sliced with cheese, cold meat or potato gratin.

MY TIP: Although it seems laborious to blanch and brine the onions, it is worth all the effort. The salty brine draws moisture from the onions so that when they are immersed in the hot spicy vinegar they immediately suck up all the infused flavours.

> **RECOMMENDED CHILLIES:** Red Bird's Eye, Cayenne, Habanero.

main dishes

Moroccan-spiced Lamb Burgers with Pickled Cucumber & Yogurt Dressing

Stracotto di Manzo, or Italian Pot Roast

Seriously Tasty Traditional Texas Chili

Roast Pork Chops with Spicy Lentils & Green Chilli Bhajis

Sweet Chilli-glazed Ham

Baked Chilli Eggs

Huevos Rancheros

Texas Marinated Steak with Stuffed Mushrooms

Provençal-style Lamb Casserole

Mango & Chilli-marinated Chicken

Baked, Goat Cheese-stuffed Chicken Breast with Chargrilled Corn-On-The-Cob

Jerk Chicken with Lime & Caramelized Pineapple

Peruvian-style Chilli & Garlic Chicken with New Potatoes

Whole Roast Salmon Stuffed with Salsa Verde Piccante

Cacciucco, or Italian Fish Stew

Creole Seafood Burritos

Spiced Scallops with Saffron Paella Rice

Dan's Creole Fish Stew

Salade Niçoise with Seared Tuna & Chilli Lemon Potatoes

Fruity African Bean Stew

Spanish Tortilla with Roasted Piquillo Peppers

Vegetable Chilli Roast with Mushroom & Tarragon Gravy

Chilli Veggie Burger with Sun-dried Tomatoes & Spicy Red Onion Relish

)))) Moroccan-spiced Lamb Burgers with Pickled Cucumber & Yogurt Dressing

I was told by a friend that a good lamb burger recipe can always be improved upon by the addition of grated apple. Try this recipe; I think it proves the theory. In fact, I found it so delicious that I added sun-dried apricots too.

sea salt and freshly ground
    black pepper
toasted pita bread, to serve
simple salad, to serve

Burgers

500 g/1 lb. minced/ground
    lamb (lean is good but a
    little fat is better as this
    helps to create a juicy
    burger)
1 small onion, finely chopped
½ small eating apple, peeled,
    cored and grated
5 sun-dried apricots, finely
    chopped
1 garlic clove, crushed
1 small red chilli, deseeded
    and finely chopped
1½ teaspoons Ras el Hanout
    (Moroccan spice blend)
1 tablespoon chilli jam/pepper
    jelly
1 tablespoon plain/all-purpose
    flour
1 tablespoon sunflower oil

Pickled cucumber & yogurt dressing

½ small red onion, thinly
    sliced
4 tablespoons plain yogurt
small handful of fresh mint,
    finely chopped
100 g/½ cup finely chopped
    Pickled Baby Cucumber
    (see page 38)
good squeeze of lemon juice

Serves 6

To make the burgers, put the lamb, onion, apple, apricots, garlic, chilli, Ras el Hanout, chilli jam/pepper jelly, 1 teaspoon salt and 1 teaspoon pepper in a large bowl. Mix everything together well by mashing it with your hands. Try to mix it evenly and thoroughly without overworking the mixture. It should now just hold together.

Divide the mixture into 6 and gently press to flatten and form generous burgers.

Place the burgers on a lightly floured tray, cover with clingfilm/plastic wrap and refrigerate for at least 1 hour. The flavours will benefit from being left to meld for longer.

Meanwhile, to make the pickled cucumber & yogurt dressing, place the sliced onion in a medium bowl, then pour over enough just-boiled water to cover. Leave for about 30 seconds. Drain and rinse the onion under cold water to refresh. Pat dry on kitchen paper/paper towels and season lightly with a little salt. Put the yogurt and mint in a small bowl and mix together thoroughly. Add the pickled cucumber, blanched onions and lemon juice and mix through the yogurt and mint mixture. Cover and refrigerate until you are ready to serve.

Just before you are ready to cook the burgers, preheat a barbecue/grill or grill/broiler to medium–hot.

Brush the sunflower oil over the burgers and barbecue/grill or grill/broil for 6–8 minutes each side or until they are cooked through.

Serve the burgers with toasted pita bread, a simple salad and a dollop of the pickled cucumber & yogurt dressing.

> **RECOMMENDED CHILLIES:** For this, a small, generic medium–hot red chilli would be ideal; I would be tempted to use a small Cherry Bomb.

)))) Stracotto di Manzo, or Italian Pot Roast

This is an Italian family favourite. We often serve it for Christmas lunch when all the preparation adds greatly to the anticipation of the meal. Although, with the marinating of the beef, this meal seems like an epic task, it is actually very simple to make. Once cooking it tends to rather look after itself, leaving you with plenty of time to think about other things, like the best wine to serve with it.

1 kg/2¼ lbs. beef (choose a lean cut of meat like rump or shoulder)

2 carrots, roughly chopped

2 celery sticks, chopped

1 large onion, chopped

1 courgette/zucchini, chopped

sprig of fresh rosemary

2 large fresh sage leaves

2 fresh bay leaves

½ tablespoon black peppercorns

3 garlic cloves, bruised and skin on

1 small, dried, hot red chilli

1 large, dried, mild red chilli, deseeded and cut in to 1-cm/⅜-inch strips

1 bottle of robust Italian red wine, eg Sangiovese or Chianti

3 tablespoons olive oil

1 tablespoon tomato purée/paste

sea salt and freshly ground black pepper

kitchen twine

stovetop casserole dish with lid

Serves 6

Put the beef in a large dish with the vegetables, herbs, peppercorns, garlic and chillies and pour the wine over everything. Cover the dish with a lid or with clingfilm/plastic wrap and refrigerate for at least 12 hours, although 24 hours is recommended. The meat should be entirely immersed in the wine. If this is not possible, turn the meat every few hours.

When the meat has finished marinating, lift it out of the dish (reserving the marinade) and allow to dry on kitchen paper/paper towels. Tie up the beef with kitchen twine to help it hold its shape during cooking, and season well with salt and pepper.

In the stovetop casserole dish, heat the oil over medium heat, then seal the beef on all sides. Once nicely browned, remove from the dish and set aside. Pass the reserved marinade through a colander into a jug/small pitcher. In the same dish over the same heat, add all the vegetables from the colander and fry for about 10 minutes. Add the tomato purée/paste and mix through. Return the beef to the pan and pour over the marinade. Bring to the boil. Reduce to low heat, cover with the lid and simmer for a minimum of 2 hours, turning the meat once or twice. It is common to cook this over very low heat for upwards of 6 hours, but if you do this you must remember to turn the meat a few times.

Remove the beef from the dish, cover with foil and set aside to rest. Discard the rosemary sprig and bay leaves. Using a hand blender, blend the remaining contents of the dish to form a gravy-like sauce. If you prefer a thicker sauce, return the dish to the heat and simmer gently until the desired consistency is achieved.

Cut the beef into thick slices and serve with roast potatoes and vegetables of your choice. Pour the sauce generously over the beef.

RECOMMENDED CHILLIES: Dried Bird's Eye, Ancho, Pasilla or milder Nu Mex chillies.

))) Seriously Tasty Traditional Texas Chili

I can't begin to emphasise the importance of a good chilli powder to the taste of your final chili. I picked up the recipe for my own Traditional Texas Chilli Powder from an 87-year-old lady in Austin, Texas. She assured me the recipe was already at least 150 years old! I think it has the perfect blend of chillies, garlic, cumin and herbs. We spent a great deal of time talking about what goes into a good chili — there really are no hard, fast rules. It is, however, interesting to note that chili con carne in its original form was as often made from venison as it was beef! If you fancy making my chilli powder yourself (and I almost insist you do) see page 134.

1.5 kg/3¼ lbs. of the best stewing steak you can get (prime boneless beef chuck)

2 tablespoons vegetable oil

3 tablespoons medium-heat Chipotle sauce

2 onions, finely chopped

4 large garlic cloves, crushed or finely chopped

3 tablespoons Dan's Traditional Texas Chilli Powder (see page 134)

chopped Cayenne chillies, preferably Ring of Fire (optional)

2 x 400-g/14-oz. cans chopped tomatoes

750 ml/3 cups hot beef or vegetable stock

140-g/6-oz. can or tube of tomato purée/paste

2 ripe yellow and/or red sweet/bell peppers, deseeded and chopped

1 tablespoon sweet paprika

1 teaspoon dried oregano, preferably Mexican

400-g/14-oz. can kidney beans

1 teaspoon ground white pepper

3–4 Jalapeños, halved lengthways and deseeded

additional hot sauce, to taste

sea salt and freshly ground black pepper

Serves 8–10

Cut the beef into even cubes and remove any sinew; leave a little fat on the meat to melt into the sauce. Heat half the oil in a heavy-bottomed saucepan over high heat, then start to brown the cubes of beef evenly. When this is nearly complete, add the Chipotle sauce. Keep the steak moving and coat in the sauce. Remove from the pan and set aside.

In the same pan, gently fry the onions and garlic with 2 tablespoons of the chilli powder and the rest of the oil until translucent. Do not allow to burn! If you wish to increase the chilli heat, add some chopped Cayenne chillies and gently soften. Add the canned tomatoes and reheat, stirring occasionally.

Return the beef to the pan with 500 ml/2 cups of the stock and the tomato purée/paste and bring gently to the boil. Reduce to a simmer, then add the sweet/bell peppers, paprika, oregano, kidney beans and white pepper. Stir well and reduce to a very gentle simmer. At this point, it is great to add the Jalapeños to float on the surface as everything cooks.

Cover and cook over low heat for at least 3 hours, stirring every so often. Add the remaining stock if it starts to look dry. 1–1½ hours before the end of cooking, add the remaining chilli powder and a generous slug of hot sauce, to taste. Season with salt and pepper.

Serve with rice, a dollop of sour cream, more hot sauce and a generous handful of grated cheddar.

MY TIP: This is a great dish to make a large batch of and then portion and freeze; as with all chilis, the flavour just gets better and better.

RECOMMENDED CHILLIES: Cayenne, Ring of Fire and Jalapeño are great for this but you can also use Ancho, Nu Mex Red and Serrano.

)))) Roast Pork Chops with Spicy Lentils & Green Chilli Bhajis

4 x 225-g/7-oz. pork loin chops

sea salt and freshly ground black pepper

Green Chilli Bhajis (see page 109), to serve

Lentils

3 tablespoons sunflower oil

1 small carrot, diced

1 celery stick, diced

50 g/2 oz. leek, diced

1 large shallot, diced

2 garlic cloves, finely chopped

1 big tablespoon chopped fresh ginger

1 green finger chilli, deseeded and finely chopped

1 bouquet garni (to make your own, see page 60)

1 tablespoon Madras curry powder

200 g/1 cup Puy lentils

400-ml/14-oz. can of coconut milk

400 ml/1⅔ cups chicken stock

2 big handfuls of baby spinach leaves

3 tablespoons chopped fresh coriander/cilantro

Raita

6 tablespoons plain yogurt

3 tablespoons finely diced cucumber flesh (no seeds)

squeeze of lemon juice

2 tablespoons chopped fresh mint

Garnish

1 small carrot, grated

1 small red onion, thinly sliced

8 fresh coriander/cilantro leaves

squeeze of lemon juice

drizzle of toasted sesame oil

Serves 4

This is the perfect dish for serving when you have friends coming round. Virtually everything can be prepared a little in advance, the kitchen will be full of the most wonderful aromatic smells, and it has enough elements to keep it exciting. The mild pork loin is very simply cooked and beautifully balanced by the lentils and (very!) spicy bhajis.

Preheat the oven to 180°C (350°F) Gas 4.

To cook the lentils, put a saucepan over low heat and add 2 tablespoons of the oil. Sweat the carrot, celery, leek and shallot for about 5 minutes, or until soft. Next add the garlic, ginger, chilli, bouquet garni and curry powder and mix. Add the lentils and cook for 3 minutes. Add the coconut milk and stock and simmer for about 30 minutes or until the lentils are cooked.

Meanwhile, heat the remaining sunflower oil in a frying pan and sear the pork chops on both sides until golden brown. Transfer to an ovenproof dish and roast in the preheated oven for about 10 minutes, or until cooked through. Let rest for about 5 minutes before serving.

To make the raita, combine all the ingredients in a small bowl and reserve in the fridge. Do the same to make the garnish.

To serve, fold the spinach and coriander/cilantro into the cooked lentils and season to taste. Serve the lentils, pork chops and green chilli bhajis with the bowls of raita and garnish alongside.

MY TIP: If you wish to add a little extra kick to the pork chops themselves, I would recommend taking 1 tablespoon of the Jamaican Jerk Marinade from page 129, mixing it with 2 tablespoons sunflower oil and with a pastry brush, lightly coating each chop with this mixture approximately 30 minutes before searing them.

RECOMMENDED CHILLIES: Indian-style green finger chillies, eg Pusa Jawala.

)))) Sweet Chilli-glazed Ham

A very simple way of feeding a lot of people, this gives a little chilli twist to a classic baked ham. For a perfect Christmas chilli feast we like to cook a ham like this, along with Stracotto di Manzo (page 55) and Whole Roast Salmon Stuffed with Salsa Verde Piccante (page 79). It provides a great array of textures and flavours and despite itself, still has a certain traditional appeal.

3–4 sprigs of fresh thyme

2 fresh bay leaves

sprig of fresh parsley

4.5-kg/10-lb. ham on the bone

1 carrot, roughly chopped

1 onion, roughly chopped

2 celery sticks, roughly chopped

7–8 black peppercorns

3 whole cloves

330-ml/12-oz. can or bottle of stout beer (eg Guinness or Mackeson)

3 tablespoons sweet chilli sauce

2 tablespoons pure maple syrup

2 tablespoons Dijon mustard

kitchen twine

stovetop casserole dish with lid

Serves 12–14

Tie the thyme, bay leaves and parsley together with kitchen twine to make a bouquet garni.

Place the ham in the casserole dish, add the bouquet garni, carrot, onion, celery, peppercorns, cloves and beer. Top up with cold water until the ham is covered. Set over medium heat and bring to the boil. Reduce the heat, partially cover with the lid and gently simmer for about 3 hours. If it starts to look dry, add only boiling water.

At the end of cooking, remove the dish from the heat and set aside for 20–30 minutes to cool with the ham still in the cooking stock.

Preheat the oven to 200°C (400°F) Gas 6.

Remove the ham from the dish and place on a large board. Cut away and discard the skin, leaving an even layer of fat exposed all over the meat. Place the ham in a large roasting pan and, with a sharp knife, score the fat in a diamond pattern, making sure not to cut through to the meat.

Mix the sweet chilli sauce, maple syrup and mustard thoroughly with a balloon whisk. Spread this glaze evenly over the ham, ensuring it is well coated. Roast the ham in the preheated oven for about 30–40 minutes until nicely browned and the glaze has formed a golden crust. Baste the meat with the glaze that runs into the roasting pan during cooking.

Let the ham rest for a few minutes before carving, then serve hot with creamy mustard mashed potato. It can also be served cold.

MY TIP: This recipe requires a good-quality sweet chilli sauce, ideally one containing a little ginger, garlic and lime juice as this will add a delicious depth of flavour as well as the gentle chilli warmth.

Alternative glazes can be made with maple syrup and Chipotle chillies (rehydrated for about 20 minutes in hot water), or with the Habanero Marmalade from page 121.

)))) Baked Chilli Eggs

This is a wonderfully warming and comforting dish – a version of 'chiles con huevos' – long associated with the long, hot days and even longer, frosty nights of the vast flat plains of the Texas Panhandle. This dish originated in the Mexican border country but is now fairly commonly found throughout the United States. Although this recipe is often cooked in a single casserole dish, in this version the mixture is divided into individual ramekins before the eggs are added, and served as a light meal. It is ideal for breakfast or as a supper treat.

25 g/2 tablespoons butter

1 garlic clove, crushed

125 g/4 oz. smoked ham, chopped

225 g/8 oz. mushrooms, diced

2 hot green chillies, finely chopped

225 ml/1 cup sour cream

2 teaspoons dried parsley

½ teaspoon dried oregano

6 eggs

200 g/2 cups grated mature/sharp cheddar

sea salt and freshly ground black pepper

toast, rubbed with a garlic clove, to serve

hot sauce, to serve

6 individual ovenproof ramekins

Serves 6 for a light meal or breakfast

Preheat the oven to 190°C (375°F) Gas 5.

Melt the butter in a heavy-based frying pan over medium heat and fry the garlic and ham for about 2 minutes, stirring regularly to prevent the garlic from burning. Add the mushrooms and chillies and continue to cook for about 5–10 minutes until the mushrooms start to brown and the chillies begin to soften. Remove from the heat and stir in the sour cream, parsley and oregano. Season lightly with salt and pepper. Divide the mixture equally between the ramekins and let stand for about 10 minutes to allow the flavours to blend.

Make a shallow hollow in each mixture and carefully break an egg into each. Season the eggs with salt and pepper. Bake in the preheated oven for about 20–25 minutes or until the egg whites have set. Remove the ramekins from the oven and sprinkle the grated cheese over all of them. Return to the oven for about 5 minutes, or until the cheese is bubbling. Serve immediately with garlicky toast and a bottle of hot sauce to splash on the eggs.

MY TIPS: If it is very warm in your kitchen, place the mixture in the fridge to set a little before making the hollows and adding the eggs.

For an even more luxurious (and meat-free) alternative, substitute the smoked ham for smoked salmon. Serve with a lightly dressed baby leaf salad.

> **RECOMMENDED CHILLIES:** Serrano, Mirasol or Espanola; Anaheim if you want it a bit milder.

)))) Huevos Rancheros

This dish is hot! It is often served for brunch with a Bloody Mary as something of a hangover cure. If you prefer it slightly milder, reduce the amount of fiery green chilli appropriately. Top it all off with your own Salsa Cruda from page 118. This is best eaten outside in the sunshine at your favourite table wearing very dark sunglasses! For the perfect mixer for the Bloody Mary, see page 154.

½ tablespoon olive oil

8 slices of back or streaky bacon, finely chopped

1 large onion, finely chopped

1 garlic clove, crushed

4 hot green chillies, finely chopped

1 mild red chilli, deseeded and finely chopped

4 tomatoes, skinned (see page 122) and roughly chopped

½ teaspoon sea salt

¼ teaspoon freshly ground black pepper

8 eggs

4 plain 20-cm/8-inch flour tortillas

Salsa Cruda (see page 118), to serve

Serves 4

Heat the oil in a frying pan and gently fry the bacon until almost cooked. Drain off all but 1 teaspoon of the fat.

Add the onion and garlic to the pan and cook, allowing to lightly brown. Add the chillies, tomatoes, salt and pepper, stir well and cover. Bring to the boil, reduce the heat and simmer for about 20 minutes, stirring frequently.

Meanwhile, fry or poach the eggs to your taste and gently warm the tortillas in a frying pan or warm oven, or under the grill/broiler.

To serve, place 2 eggs per person on a warmed tortilla and liberally spoon the salsa cruda over the eggs. Eat immediately!

RECOMMENDED CHILLIES: For the hot chillies – Green Cayenne, Ring of Fire, Thai Hot. For the mild chilli – Nu Mex or Guajillo.

Texas Marinated Steak with Stuffed Mushrooms

2 x 225-g/7-oz. rump or bottom round steaks

1 tablespoon sunflower oil

sea salt and freshly ground black pepper

Marinade

75 ml/⅓ cup dry red wine

1 tablespoon muscovado/raw cane or light brown sugar

1 tablespoon white wine vinegar

1 teaspoon crushed Chipotle chilli

1 tablespoon groundnut oil

1 red sweet/bell pepper, deseeded and finely chopped

2 large ripe tomatoes, skinned (see page 122), deseeded and finely chopped

1 teaspoon Dan's Traditional Texas Chilli Powder (see page 134)

2 garlic cloves, crushed

¼ teaspoon sweet smoked paprika (pimentón dulce)

½ teaspoon ground white pepper

Stuffed mushrooms

2 large field mushrooms

1 teaspoon olive oil

75 g/2½ oz. Roquefort cheese

2 tablespoons crème fraîche or cream cheese

sprig of fresh rosemary, leaves finely chopped

25 g/2 tablespoons butter

1 garlic clove, crushed

dash of Worcestershire sauce

2–3 tablespoons breadcrumbs

Serves 2

> **RECOMMENDED CHILLIES:**
> Jalapeño or Serrano.

Lots of rich, bold flavours combine here to create a great dish for a special occasion. The marinated steak will have delicious smoky undertones balanced with a slightly sweet fruitiness from the red pepper and tomatoes. This combines wonderfully with the Roquefort cheese used to stuff the mushrooms.

To make the marinade, gently warm the red wine in a small saucepan, add the sugar and stir to dissolve. Add the vinegar and crushed Chipotle to the pan and remove from the heat. Set aside for about 20 minutes to rehydrate the chipotle. After 20 minutes, place ½ teaspoon salt and the remaining marinade ingredients in a food processor, add the wine mixture and pulse until as smooth as possible. Add a little water if it is too stiff. Put the steaks in a bowl and rub the marinade into them thoroughly. Cover and refrigerate for at least 2 hours.

When you are ready to start cooking, preheat the oven to 200°C (400°F) Gas 6.

To make the stuffed mushrooms, remove the stalks from the mushrooms and finely chop. Rub the caps of the mushrooms with the olive oil and season well with salt and pepper. Place, cap side down, in a small roasting dish. In a bowl, mash the Roquefort, crème fraîche and rosemary to a paste. Use this to stuff the cavities of the mushrooms.

Heat half the butter in a small frying pan and add the chopped mushroom stalks. Fry for a few moments, then add the garlic and Worcestershire sauce. Continue cooking gently until the garlic has softened. Spread this mixture over the cheese stuffing and sprinkle the breadcrumbs over the top. Place a small knob of the remaining butter on the breadcrumbs on each mushroom and bake in the preheated oven for about 15 minutes, or until the cheese in bubbling through the mushroom and garlic layer.

Remove the steak from the marinade, draining the excess marinade back into the bowl and reserving it. Pat the steaks dry on kitchen paper/paper towels. Heat the sunflower oil in the frying pan over high heat. Fry the steaks for 2 minutes each side, then pour the reserved marinade into the pan. Allow to come to the boil, then reduce the heat. Simmer until the marinade is cooked through and has reduced a little. Remove the steaks and set aside to rest for 2 minutes, then slice diagonally into thick slices. Dress with the reduced marinade and serve with a stuffed mushroom.

Provençal-style Lamb Casserole

During the hot summer months in the south of France, the hillside banks of wild herbs take a real pounding from the intense Provençal sunshine. When they are picked and dried this lack of moisture produces the intensely flavoured herbs that we love to associate with this region. It is interesting to note that when air-drying herbs (and chillies for that matter) pruning a fairly sizeable side branch laden with leaves or fruit and hanging it upside down to dry encourages the essential flavouring oils in these plants to be drawn into the leaves or fruit, replacing the water content as they dehydrate. This is the best way of retaining a full depth of flavour in your dried herbs. When they are added to cooking, these oils are soon released, adding both flavour and fragrance to the dish.

1 kg/2¼ lbs. lamb leg meat (fat removed), cut into 2.5–3 cm/1-inch cubes

2 tablespoons olive oil

1 large onion, chopped

3 carrots, roughly chopped

3 large garlic cloves, crushed

2 large tomatoes, skinned (see page 122), deseeded and chopped

1 tablespoon Provençal Herb Blend (see page 135)

500 ml/2 cups hot lamb, chicken or vegetable stock

400-g/14-oz. can butter beans

1 medium–hot red chilli, deseeded and cut into strips

1–2 tablespoons cornflour/cornstarch (optional)

sea salt and freshly ground black pepper

Marinade

2 fat sprigs of fresh rosemary

3 fresh bay leaves

6 juniper berries

1 celery stick, chopped

2 strips of orange zest

1 bottle of dry Côtes du Rhône red wine

stovetop casserole dish/ Dutch oven

Serves 4

Put all the marinade ingredients in a small, heavy-based saucepan over medium heat and bring to the boil. Reduce the heat and simmer for about 20 minutes until the contents have reduced by about half. Strain the marinade into a large bowl and set aside to cool until nearly room temperature.

Place the lamb pieces in the marinade, cover and refrigerate for at least 2 hours.

Heat the oil in the stovetop casserole dish/Dutch oven over medium heat. Remove the lamb from the marinade (reserving the marinade) and add to the hot oil. Fry, stirring constantly, until evenly browned – about 5 minutes. Remove the meat from the dish and set aside.

Fry the onion in the same pan for about 2 minutes, then add the carrots and garlic. Fry for a further 3 minutes. Add the tomatoes, Provençal herb blend and reserved marinade and season with salt and pepper. Bring the mixture back to the boil, then add the lamb pieces and stock. Return to the boil, reduce the heat and add the beans and chilli. Simmer for 30–35 minutes, uncovered, or until the lamb is tender.

Serve in large bowls with boiled new potatoes or fresh garlic bread.

MY TIP: About 10 minutes before cooking is complete, take a tablespoon or 2 of the stock from the pan and mix with the cornflour/cornstarch to form a paste. Stir this paste back into the casserole. This will slightly thicken the casserole over the last few minutes of cooking.

> **RECOMMENDED CHILLIES:** Piment d'Espelette or any other medium-heat bullet-style red chilli, such as a standard supermarket red.

))) Mango & Chilli-marinated Chicken

This dish creates wonderful exotic flavours by combining the smooth sweetness of mango and some quite traditional Indian spicing. I love mango in marinades: apart from being delicious in its own right, it carries other flavours so well and has great tenderizing properties. In this recipe we cook the chicken in the marinade, turning it into something of a cook-in sauce. This works well with homemade marinades as they tend not to have the acidity (needed to extend shelf life) of storebought versions.

1 teaspoon mixed peppercorns

1 teaspoon coriander seeds

½ teaspoon cumin seeds

1 teaspoon fenugreek seeds

½ teaspoon fennel seeds

1 teaspoon sea salt

200 g/6½ oz. fresh mango flesh, diced (from 1 mango, about 300 g/10 oz.)

4 tablespoons white wine vinegar

4 teaspoons sugar

1 small Habanero or other very hot chilli, very finely chopped

2 garlic cloves, crushed

handful of fresh coriander/ cilantro, chopped

1–2 tablespoons olive oil, if required

4 large skinless free-range chicken breasts

pilaf rice, to serve

Green Chilli Bhajis (see page 109), to serve

Caramelized Lime, Mint & Yogurt Dip (see page 109), to serve

deep casserole dish

Serves 4

Toast the spices in a hot, dry frying pan over medium heat until the seeds start to pop. Grind them, together with the salt, using a pestle and mortar. Put the ground spices, mango, vinegar, sugar, chilli, garlic and coriander/cilantro into a food processor and blend for about 30 seconds, or until smooth. If required, loosen the marinade with 1–2 tablespoons olive oil.

Lightly score the chicken breasts with a sharp knife, place them into a deep bowl and cover with the marinade. Use your hands to rub the marinade well into the meat. Cover and refrigerate for at least 2 hours. This can be done first thing in the morning and left to marinate until the evening.

A few minutes before you are ready to start cooking, preheat the oven to 180°C (350°F) Gas 4.

Place the chicken and its marinade in the deep casserole dish, cover with foil and cook in the preheated oven for 30 minutes. Remove the foil and return the chicken to the oven for a further 10 minutes, or until cooked through.

Serve on a bed of pilaf rice with green chilli bhajis and caramelized lime, mint & yogurt dip.

MY TIP: This marinade will also work very well with salmon fillets or even pork cutlets and can be cooked in the same way, adjusting your cooking time appropriately for your chosen ingredients.

RECOMMENDED CHILLIES: Fatali, Scotch Bonnet, Datil or failing that, any Habanero variety.

)))) Baked, Goat Cheese-stuffed Chicken Breast with Chargrilled Corn-On-The-Cob

This quick and easy recipe is ideal for dinner parties. The stuffing of goat cheese and the prosciutto wrap give the simple chicken breast additional textures and depth of flavour. The cheese can be substituted for simple cheddar or Gruyère to create a really grown-up AND child-friendly feast!

2 skinless free-range chicken breasts

50 g/2 oz. firm goat cheese, grated

1 red Cayenne or other hot red chilli, deseeded and finely chopped

small handful of fresh coriander/cilantro, chopped

1 shallot, very finely chopped

2 large slices of prosciutto

olive oil, for greasing

2 corn cobs/ears of corn

sea salt and freshly ground black pepper

mixed salad, to serve

Green Pepper, Tomato & Habanero Chilli Salsa (see page 118), to serve (optional)

cocktail sticks/toothpicks

ovenproof frying pan

ridged stovetop grill pan

Serves 2

Preheat the oven to 190°C (375°F) Gas 5.

Take a sharp knife and form a cavity in the side of the chicken breasts by cutting lengthways from one end to the other.

In a bowl, combine the cheese, chilli, coriander/cilantro and shallot and mix well. Carefully stuff each chicken breast with the cheese mixture by pressing it into the chicken cavity with a teaspoon. Skewer the open side of each chicken breast with cocktail sticks/toothpicks to prevent the stuffing from escaping. Lightly season each chicken breast with salt and pepper, then wrap a slice of prosciutto around each one.

Lightly grease the ovenproof frying pan with olive oil and heat. Sear the chicken in the pan until golden brown on both sides. Transfer the pan to the preheated oven and cook for 20–25 minutes or until the chicken is thoroughly cooked through.

A few minutes before the chicken has finished cooking, put the corn in a pan of boiling salted water, wait for the water to return to the boil, then cook for 2–3 minutes.

Preheat the ridged stovetop grill pan. Remove the corn from the pan and drain. Toss the corn in a tablespoon of olive oil and season with salt and pepper, ensuring that it is evenly coated. Lightly char the corn in the hot pan so that so it caramelizes a little.

When the chicken has finished cooking, let rest for 5 minutes.

Serve the chicken and corn with a mixed salad and/or the green pepper, tomato & Habanero chilli salsa.

> **RECOMMENDED CHILLIES:** Cayenne, Piccante di Cayenna, Ring of Fire, Long Slim.

//// Jerk Chicken with Lime & Caramelized Pineapple

Jerk is a style of cooking native to the Caribbean island of Jamaica. Traditionally chicken or pork were marinated in a mixture of ground pimento berries and Scotch Bonnet chillies, then cooked and smoked in equal proportion over a fire of pimento wood to which the leaves and berries were also added. This gave the meat a very distinctive taste. In more modern times (and outside the Caribbean) the term 'jerk' refers more to the marinade used to flavour and tenderize the meat prior to cooking.

4 free-range chicken breasts, skin on

150 ml/⅔ cup Jamaican Jerk Marinade (see page 129)

1 lime, ½ thinly sliced and ½ freshly squeezed

1 tablespoon dark rum

1 teaspoon dark soy sauce

1 teaspoon dark brown sugar

½ pineapple, peeled, cored and cut into wedges

groundnut oil, for greasing (optional)

Green Pepper, Tomato & Habanero Chilli Salsa (see page 118), to serve

rice salad, to serve

ridged stovetop grill pan (optional)

Serves 4

Put the chicken in a bowl and cover with the Jamaican jerk marinade. Make sure the chicken is thoroughly coated, then cover and marinate in the refrigerator for at least 2 hours; overnight is ideal.

Remove the chicken from the marinade (reserve the marinade). Gently lift the edge of the skin on each chicken breast, creating a small pocket against the flesh. Take 1–2 thin slices of lime (1 for a small piece of chicken, and 2 for a large) and slide these under the skin. These will caramelize during cooking.

You can roast, griddle or barbecue/grill the chicken. If roasting, preheat the oven to 190°C (375°F) Gas 5. Put the chicken in a roasting dish. Spoon a few tablespoons of the marinade over the chicken. Roast in the preheated oven for about 35–40 minutes or until fully cooked and the juices run clear. Baste the chicken with the marinade as it roasts. The chicken will become quite dark in places while cooking; this is normal but if you wish to avoid it, cover the pan with foil for the first 25 minutes of cooking.

If cooking on a ridged stovetop grill pan, heat the pan, adding a little groundnut oil if you like. Once hot, sear the chicken on both sides, then lower the heat and cook for about 8–10 minutes each side.

On the barbecue/grill, over medium heat, the chicken should take about 10 minutes each side; the juices in the middle should run clear.

If barbecuing or griddling, baste with the marinade several times during cooking. Please note that this marinade was in contact with uncooked chicken, so always allow 5–10 minutes between the last time you baste and the end of cooking to ensure the marinade itself is thoroughly cooked.

Mix the lime juice, rum, soy sauce and sugar in a bowl and add the pineapple wedges. Mix to coat thoroughly. Remove the wedges from this mixture, paint with a little groundnut oil and place on a hot stovetop grill pan or on the barbecue to lightly and evenly char.

Serve the chicken with the caramelized pineapple, green pepper, tomato & Habanero chilli salsa and a rice salad.

))) Peruvian-style Chilli & Garlic Chicken with New Potatoes

South-American chillies like the large red Rocoto from Peru are amongst the earliest chillies to have been cultivated by man. It is believed that the Andean peoples were growing Rocoto (or Locoto in Bolivia) 5000 years ago. They are part of the 'Capsicum pubescens' family of chillies, meaning that the leaves and stems are remarkably hairy! The Rocoto has thick skin and flesh rather like a sweet/bell pepper but is smaller and very hot. Unusually its seeds are virtually black. For a chilli plant, it is surprisingly hardy and often grows at considerable altitudes in the Andes. Fortunately it also tastes delicious and, as below, is found in many classic South-American dishes.

800 g–1 kg/1¾–2¼ lbs. small/
    medium waxy new potatoes,
    washed and cut into even
    sizes

25 g/2 tablespoons butter

6 large skinless free-range
    chicken breasts

2 slices of lemon

2 fresh bay leaves

200 ml/¾ cup hot light
    vegetable or chicken stock

120 ml/½ cup sunflower oil

3 onions, chopped

6 garlic cloves, crushed

4 Rocoto chillies, deseeded
    and finely chopped

450 g/1 lb. (about 3 cups)
    roasted unsalted peanuts,
    roughly chopped

½ teaspoon ground cinnamon

120 g/1½ cups finely grated
    hard cheese, eg Parmesan

1 tablespoon cumin seeds,
    crushed

180 ml/¾ cup plain yogurt,
    at room temperature

sea salt and freshly ground
    black pepper

wilted spinach, to serve

Serves 6

Boil the potatoes in a pan of lightly salted water for 15–20 minutes until they are nearly cooked but still a little firm. Drain and set aside in the pan with the lid on.

Meanwhile, heat the butter in a wok-style frying pan or sauté pan over medium heat. Gently fry the chicken breasts until they are sealed and slightly browned. Add the lemon slices, bay leaves and stock and season with salt and pepper. Cover and bring to a simmer. Cook for about 20 minutes, or until the chicken is just cooked but still moist.

Remove the pan from the heat. Lift the chicken out of the pan, wrap in foil to retain moistness and set aside. Leaving the stock in the pan, return to the heat. Add the nearly cooked new potatoes, turn the heat up to medium/high and continue to cook, uncovered, for about 15 minutes, tossing frequently until the remaining liquid has evaporated from the pan. Remove the pan from the heat, fish out the bay leaves and discard. There is no need to remove the lemon slices as they will have softened and will taste delicious. Cover the pan and set aside.

Heat the oil in a large saucepan. Add the onions and garlic and cook gently over very low heat for about 5 minutes, or until softened. Add the chillies, peanuts, cinnamon, cheese and cumin and mix together. Cook for 5 minutes.

Meanwhile, unwrap the cooked chicken and tear into generous strips. Add to the peanut mixture, stir in the yogurt and season with salt and pepper. Gently heat through. Serve with the deliciously flavoured sautéed potatoes and maybe some simple wilted spinach.

> **RECOMMENDED CHILLIES:** Rocoto, Manzano, Aji Limo. If these traditional South-American varieties are not available, Jalapeño or even standard hot green chillies could work equally well.

Whole Roast Salmon Stuffed with Salsa Verde Piccante

sea salt and freshly ground
  black pepper

Salsa verde piccante

handful of fresh flat leaf
  parsley, chopped

2½ tablespoons finely chopped
  wild garlic leaves (optional)

small handful of fresh basil,
  torn

a few fresh mint leaves,
  chopped

2–3 tablespoons capers

grated zest of 1 lemon

1 small, hot green chilli,
  deseeded and finely
  chopped

6 anchovy fillets, drained,
  rinsed and chopped

1 garlic clove, crushed

1 tablespoon extra virgin
  olive oil

Whole roast salmon

2 beef tomatoes, sliced

1 fennel bulb, thinly sliced

1 tablespoon capers

1 fresh bay leaf

2 garlic cloves, sliced

grated zest of ½ lemon

½ teaspoon dried chilli/
  red pepper flakes

2 large sprigs of fresh thyme

3 tablespoons extra virgin
  olive oil

50 ml/3 tablespoons dry white
  wine

1 teaspoon Pastis, Pernod or
  Ricard (optional)

2.7-kg/6-lb. salmon, scaled
  and filleted, skin on (ask
  your fishmonger to do this
  for you)

*baking sheet about 40 x 28 cm/
  16 x 11 inches, lined with
  greaseproof/parchment paper*

Serves 6–8

A few years ago I saw a version of this dish being cooked by English chef Rick Stein on one of his fabulous cookery series. It immediately became a favourite in our household and over the years has evolved to become something that we love so much that we prepared it for our wedding guests. It was a great pleasure to cook for everyone who had travelled all the way to Northumberland and it seemed fitting to serve this dish within earshot of the South Tyne, one of the UK's great salmon rivers.

Preheat the oven to 220°C (425°F) Gas 7.

Put all the ingredients for the salsa verde piccante into a large mortar and mash to a rough paste with the pestle. Alternatively, use a food processor and pulse briefly for a few seconds. Season with a little salt and pepper, if required.

To make the whole roast salmon, arrange the tomato and fennel slices over the prepared baking sheet to make a bed for the salmon. Scatter the capers, bay leaf, garlic, half the lemon zest and half the chilli/red pepper flakes over the bed. Lay the sprigs of thyme on top. Whisk together the oil, wine, Pastis, if using, and 3 tablespoons water, then pour over the bed.

Take one of the salmon fillets and season both sides with a little salt and pepper. Lay the fillet, skin side down, on the tomato/fennel bed. Spread the salsa verde piccante evenly over the exposed flesh of the fillet. Season the other fillet and lay this on top of the salsa verde, flesh side down. With a pastry brush, paint the uppermost skin side of the salmon with some of the oil mixture that has seeped out onto the paper from the tomato/fennel bed and scatter the rest of the lemon zest and chilli/red pepper flakes over the top. Generously season with salt and pepper. If the fish is a little large for the baking sheet, arrange diagonally or fold the tail around slightly.

Roast in the preheated oven for about 30 minutes. The skin will go slightly brown and begin to crisp. Remove from the oven and let rest for 15 minutes. Serve with the tomato and fennel mixture. It works well with new potatoes, salad and Fresh Aïoli (page 117). It's also delicious cold.

> **RECOMMENDED CHILLIES:** Any small, hot, green Cayenne for the salsa.

Cacciucco, or Italian Fish Stew

Originating in Livorno on the Tuscan coast of Italy, this fish stew encapsulates everything that is best about Italian cooking. Cacciucco is hearty, robust, seasonal and tastes wonderful. It speaks volumes about the ingredients and very little about the chef! Its seasonality also makes it very cost effective to cook. See 'My Tip' at the bottom of the recipe for suggestions on the types of seafood to use.

1 kg/2¼ lbs. assorted fresh seafood – use whatever is in season; this dish should not be expensive and should include whole (scaled and gutted) fish and shellfish

85 ml/⅓ cup olive oil

1 onion, finely chopped

1 carrot, finely chopped

1 celery stick including leaves, finely chopped

3 garlic cloves, crushed

2 fresh bay leaves

sprig of fresh thyme

250 ml/1 cup red wine

4 plum tomatoes, skinned (see page 122) and chopped

500 ml/2 cups light fish or chicken stock

1 hot chilli, deseeded and finely chopped

sea salt and freshly ground black pepper

handful of fresh flat leaf parsley, finely chopped

Croutons

6 slices of Italian bread

1 garlic clove, peeled

stovetop casserole dish, heavy-based saucepan or Dutch oven

Serves 6

Clean the fish, remove the heads and put them aside. Your fishmonger will do this for you if you ask him/her nicely. Cut any large fish into 6–8-cm/3-inch chunks. You can leave small fish whole. Season the fish with salt and pepper.

Heat half the oil in the stovetop casserole dish, heavy-based saucepan or Dutch oven. Fry the onion for 2 minutes. Add the carrot and celery and fry for a further 2 minutes. Add the garlic, bay leaves, thyme and larger fish heads. Cook for about 5 minutes or until the fish heads have browned.

Add the red wine and bring to the boil. Reduce to a simmer and cook until the wine has reduced by half. Add the tomatoes and stock. Bring the liquid up to a simmer and cook for about 30 minutes.

Remove the pan from the heat, discard the fish heads, bay leaves and thyme sprig and briefly blend the ingredients with a hand blender to thicken. Alternatively, let cool for a few minutes, then transfer to a blender and blend. Return the sauce to the pan. Add the chilli and season with salt and pepper.

Return the pan to the heat and add the fish. Hold back any shellfish, including prawns/shrimp, until the last moment, as they will only take a matter of minutes to cook. Add half the remaining olive oil to the pan. Gently simmer for 15 minutes to cook the fish, adding any shellfish for the last 2 minutes of cooking. Stir through most of the chopped parsley and remove from the heat.

To make the croutons, heat the remaining oil in a large frying pan, then fry the slices of bread until golden. Rub each slice with the peeled clove of garlic.

When you are ready to serve, drop a crouton into each bowl and ladle the cacciucco over the top. Garnish with the remaining parsley.

RECOMMENDED CHILLIES: Piccante di Cayenna or Ring of Fire.

)))) Creole Seafood Burritos

This is another wonderfully simple dish that is great for the whole family. It is mild and child-friendly but can easily be made 'dad friendly' with the simple addition of some hot salsa or even a few finely chopped Ring of Fire chillies at the end of cooking. We love to cook this on the beach at the end of a long day when nobody really wants to go home. It's always worth throwing a few useful ingredients in a cold bag when you go out for the day – there is nothing worse than having to cut a perfect day short because everyone's hungry!

25 g/2 tablespoons butter

1 onion, chopped

2 garlic cloves, finely sliced

½ teaspoon ground Ancho or other dried chilli

1 teaspoon Creole spice blend

225 g/8 oz. cooked/lump white crabmeat

125 g/4 oz. peeled cooked prawns/shrimp, chopped

100 g/1 cup grated Gruyère cheese

6 plain 25-cm/10-inch flour tortillas

sour cream, to serve

Green Pepper, Tomato & Habanero Chilli Salsa (see page 118), to serve

sea salt and freshly ground black pepper

shredded lettuce leaves, to serve

Serves 6

Heat the butter in a large frying pan, then gently fry the onion for 3 minutes. Add the garlic, chilli and Creole spice blend and cook for 10 minutes over low heat until soft, stirring to prevent the mixture from sticking.

Reduce the heat and stir in the crab and prawns/shrimp. Gently heat through and then season with salt and pepper to taste. Stir in the grated Gruyère cheese.

To serve, put a generous tablespoon of the seafood mixture onto a tortilla. Add, in equal quantities, a dollop of sour cream and one of the green pepper, tomato & Habanero chilli salsa. Add a little shredded lettuce for crunch. Fold the tortilla up over the bottom of the mixture and roll the sides around the seafood mixture. Leave the top open if you are eating immediately. Repeat with the remaining tortillas and serve.

MY TIP: These burritos are a favourite of both my boys but instead of serving with hot salsa, they like some mild guacamole and some finely chopped celery for extra crunch.

Spiced Scallops with Saffron Paella Rice

1 tablespoon olive oil

freshly squeezed juice of
½ lime

roughly chopped coriander/
cilantro, to garnish

Spiced scallops

2 tablespoons Smoked Chilli &
Rosemary Oil (see page 130)
or other hot chilli oil

2 teaspoons muscovado or
light brown sugar

3 tablespoons soy sauce

1 garlic clove, crushed

finely grated zest of 1 lemon

12 large scallops, cleaned and
deveined

Saffron paella rice

good pinch of saffron strands

1 litre/4 cups hot chicken or
vegetable stock

2 tablespoons olive oil

150 g/5 oz. chorizo sausage,
thinly sliced

2 large shallots, finely
chopped

3 garlic cloves, crushed

1 teaspoon sweet smoked
paprika (pimentón dulce)

1 teaspoon dried Guindilla or
other chilli/red pepper
flakes

500 g/2½ cups paella rice

125 ml/½ cup white wine

200 g/6½ oz. raw, peeled
prawns/shrimp

small handful of fresh flat leaf
parsley, chopped

sea salt and freshly ground
black pepper

Serves 4

When I was growing up, I can remember paella as possibly my favourite meal. The rice was exotic and wonderfully flavoured – so far removed from the over-boiled, plain rice of school; and the idea of liberally scattering seafood and sausage throughout was just too brilliant! Every mouthful was a new combination of flavours – a mini taste sensation. Quite a few years on and scallops now just sneak in as my favourite occasional treat, so in this recipe the two come together in a celebration of Mediterranean 'good taste'.

To make the spiced scallops, put the smoked chilli & rosemary oil, sugar, soy sauce, garlic and lemon zest in a bowl and whisk together. Add the scallops and mix to ensure that they are well coated. Cover and refrigerate for 30 minutes.

Meanwhile, to make the saffron paella rice, put the saffron strands in the hot stock and set aside to infuse.

Heat the oil in a large frying pan and fry the chorizo for 5 minutes, or until it is well browned and starting to go crispy. Add the shallots and garlic and fry until they begin to soften, then add the paprika and the dried chilli/red pepper flakes and cook for 30 seconds. Add the rice and cook for a further minute, tossing it to get it nicely coated.

Add the wine and saffron-infused stock. Simmer, uncovered, over medium heat for about 20 minutes, stirring occasionally. Add more hot water during cooking should the rice appear to be becoming too dry. Test the rice to see if it is cooked. If it needs a little more time, return to low heat for another 5 minutes. 2–3 minutes before cooking is complete add the prawns/shrimp and stir through. Season with salt and pepper and stir through the parsley.

Heat the olive oil in a frying pan over medium heat. Remove the scallops from the marinade and fry for 1–2 minutes each side, depending on size. Season with a little salt and pepper and lime juice.

Serve 3 scallops on top of each bed of paella and garnish with coriander/cilantro. This works well with a fresh, citrusy tomato salsa.

> **RECOMMENDED CHILLIES:** Guindilla are found throughout Spain and most commonly made into 'ristras', or strings of dried chillies. They have a medium heat and strong red colour. If they are unavailable, general-purpose, medium-heat dried chilli/red pepper flakes can be used in their place.

)))) Dan's Creole Fish Stew

Cajun and Creole cooking are all about 'joie de vivre' and one-pot ingenuity! Creole cuisine was heavily influenced by Spanish and Italian cooking; this was further developed by the introduction of Caribbean cooking techniques and Native American ingredients. Cajun cuisine was on the other hand much simpler; a joyous adaptation of the indigenous foods of the swamps and bayous of southern Louisiana. Bring them together and you get astonishingly rich, full-bodied flavours from simple ingredients.

1 kg/2¼ lbs. meaty, firm fish, preferably monkfish but salmon, red snapper, rockfish, swordfish or large prawns/shrimp also work

knob of butter

1 onion, finely chopped

3 large fleshy tomatoes, skinned (see page 122) and chopped

2 garlic cloves, crushed

2 sprigs of fresh thyme

1 fresh bay leaf

600 ml/2½ cups fish stock (or chicken or vegetable stock)

1 teaspoon sweet paprika

1 Habanero chilli, deseeded and chopped (add another chilli if you like more heat)

1 red sweet/bell pepper, finely chopped

1 green sweet/bell pepper, finely chopped

sea salt and freshly ground black pepper

basmati rice, to serve

Marinade

3 teaspoons Cajun spice blend

3 tablespoons sunflower oil

1 tablespoon honey

1 tablespoon red wine vinegar

freshly squeezed juice of ½ lime

¼ teaspoon ground cinnamon

½ teaspoon dried oregano

1 teaspoon Tabasco or Louisiana Hot Sauce

stovetop casserole dish

Serves 4–6

To make the marinade, combine the Cajun spice blend, 2 tablespoons of the sunflower oil, the honey, vinegar, lime juice, cinnamon, oregano and hot sauce in a large bowl. Mix well. Cut the fish into 2.5-cm/1-inch slices or cubes but leave any prawns/shrimp whole. Turn in the marinade to coat. Cover and refrigerate for 1–2 hours.

Now heat the remaining tablespoon of oil and the butter in the stovetop casserole dish. Gently fry the onion until softened but not brown. Add the tomatoes, garlic, thyme and bay leaf. Heat through and simmer gently for 10 minutes.

Add the stock, paprika and chilli. Habanero chillies are extremely hot, so if you're in any doubt, add it little by little, to taste! Bring to the boil, then simmer, uncovered, over low heat for about 1 hour.

Add the marinated fish, along with the marinade and half the red and green sweet/bell peppers to the sauce. Stir well.

Simmer gently, uncovered, for 10–15 minutes until the fish is cooked through. Add the remaining peppers and mix through 5 minutes before the cooking is complete. Season with salt and pepper.

Remove the bay leaf and any large thyme sprigs before serving. Serve with basmati rice or fresh baguette. I also like to finely chop some more Habanero for the adventurous diners to sprinkle on their stew; it smells great!

MY TIPS: We often make this recipe with 4 Habanero chillies – you do need to know your guests before you try this though!

For a great barbecue/grill recipe, make the marinade as above and use to coat cubed fish or chicken. Refrigerate for 1–2 hours, then skewer and barbecue/grill for fantastic, healthy kebabs/kabobs.

> **RECOMMENDED CHILLIES:** Habanero, Antillais Caribbean, Trinidad Congo, Fatali, Scotch Bonnet.

Salade Niçoise with Seared Tuna & Chilli Lemon Potatoes

I think this is the best way to eat fresh tuna. There is a lot of disagreement about what should be in a 'Salade Niçoise', but few would argue with the fact that it should have bold flavours and be representative of the best produce of the south of France. The chilli and lemon here add another dimension. All in all the salad provides a perfect foil for the seared fish while remaining true to the regional roots of the dish.

4 small, fresh tuna steaks

Chilli Lemon Potatoes

500-600 g/1¼ lbs. small new
   potatoes, scrubbed

5 tablespoons extra virgin
   olive oil, plus extra for frying

freshly squeezed juice of
   1 large lemon

1 small hot red chilli, deseeded
   and very finely chopped

1 small red onion, very finely
   chopped

sea salt flakes and freshly
   ground black pepper

Salad

4 free-range eggs

350 g/12 oz. cherry tomatoes

200 g/6½ oz. fine green beans,
   trimmed

120 g/4 oz. Niçoise olives

2 tablespoons caperberries,
   washed and dried

5–6 Baby Gem lettuces, (or
   3 Baby Romaine lettuces)
   quartered

chopped fresh flat leaf parsley

snipped fresh chives

torn fresh basil leaves

16 marinated anchovy fillets

Dressing

1 garlic clove, crushed

1 tablespoon red wine vinegar

3 tablespoons extra virgin
   olive oil

1 teaspoon Dijon mustard

squeeze of lemon juice

Serves 4

To make the chilli lemon potatoes, cook the potatoes in a saucepan of lightly salted boiling water for about 15 minutes, or until tender. Drain the water and leave the potatoes in the pan. Gently press them against the side of the pan with the back of a spoon to squash slightly. Add the oil, lemon juice, chilli and onion, replace the lid and shake the pan vigorously to thoroughly coat with the mixture. Season with salt flakes and plenty of black pepper, replace the lid and shake again. Let cool.

To make the salad, gently boil the eggs in a small pan of salted water for about 7–10 minutes depending on the size of the egg. The yolks should ideally be just soft or even slightly runny. Remove from the heat and run the eggs under cold water. Shell them and let cool completely.

Heat a small pan over high heat and add a little olive oil. Add the tomatoes and cook, moving constantly, until they begin to blister. Remove from the heat, lightly season and let cool. Boil the green beans in a small pan of boiling water for about 5 minutes, or until 'al dente'. Drain and run under cold water. Pat dry on kitchen paper/paper towels. Put the tomatoes, beans, olives, caperberries, lettuce and herbs into a large bowl.

Whisk all the dressing ingredients in a small bowl with a balloon whisk. Pour two-thirds of the dressing onto the salad mixture in the large bowl and very gently toss together until everything is well coated. Cut the eggs into quarters, add to the bowl and stir through very gently.

Put the anchovy fillets in the remaining dressing and, without mashing, press firmly with the back of a fork to flavour the dressing. Set aside.

Season the tuna well. Heat a tablespoon of olive oil in a small non-stick frying pan over medium heat. Sear the tuna for 3–4 minutes each side without stirring – do not overcook otherwise it will get dry. Remove from the heat and let rest for a few moments. Cut into thick slices. Put the salad, potatoes and tuna in 4 bowls. Remove the anchovies from the remaining dressing and arrange in the bowls. Dress with the remaining dressing.

> **RECOMMENDED CHILLIES:** Any small, hot, thin-skinned red chilli, eg Ring of Fire, Thai Hot or even a small red Bird's Eye would do well.

))))) Fruity African Bean Stew

A fruity, feisty and flavoursome bean stew, this dish is a firm favourite among all our friends: vegetarians and devout meat-eaters alike! The Baharat spice blend we use for this recipe is found in one form or another all through the Middle East and north Africa; finding one that contains allspice berries gives this dish a distinctly Moroccan feel. Although indigenous to South America, quinoa is now widely grown in Africa; it is high in protein, calcium and iron. Strangely it contains a near-perfect balance of all eight amino acids essential for human tissue development. This is a great dish to cook for parties when you aren't really sure how many people you may end up feeding!

200 g/1 cup red split lentils

100 g/⅔ cup quinoa

1 teaspoon Baharat (or similar North African) spice blend

1 tablespoon olive oil

2 onions, chopped

6 garlic cloves, crushed

2 x 400-g/14-oz. cans chopped tomatoes

600 ml/2½ cups good vegetable stock

3 tablespoons African-style hot chilli or pepper sauce

2 fresh bay leaves

generous sprig of fresh thyme

75 g/½ cup chopped dried apricots

75 g/½ cup sultanas/golden raisins

hot red chillies, chopped – as many as you like!

2 x 400-g/14-oz. cans mixed beans, drained

400-g/14-oz. can chickpeas, drained

2 ripe red sweet/bell peppers, deseeded and cut into strips

sea salt and freshly ground black pepper

couscous, to serve

stovetop casserole dish with lid

Serves 8+

Thoroughly rinse the lentils and quinoa and put in a saucepan of boiling unsalted water.

Reduce the heat to a gentle simmer and add the Baharat spice blend. Cook, uncovered, for 20 minutes, or until thick. Drain well.

Heat the oil in the stovetop casserole dish and gently fry the onions and garlic until softened but not brown.

Add the chopped tomatoes and the cooked lentils and quinoa. Stir well.

Add the vegetable stock and bring back to a gentle simmer.

Add the African-style hot sauce, bay leaves, thyme, apricots, sultanas/golden raisins, chillies, mixed beans, chickpeas and sweet/bell peppers. Stir well. Bring to the boil, then reduce the heat to a very gentle simmer and cook, covered, for at least 1 hour. Stir occasionally.

Add more stock if it looks too dry, but allow the sauce to thicken. Season with salt and pepper at the end of cooking.

Serve with couscous, brown rice or fresh bread.

MY TIP: For a truly authentic flavour, finely dice 2 Fatali chillies and present in a separate dish on the table for braver guests to sprinkle over their stew. These super-hot Habanero chillies originate from central Africa and have an amazing aroma when fresh. When you sprinkle them on top of the steaming stew at the table, the heat releases even more of their amazing fragrance and flavour while losing none of the health benefits that may be compromised by adding during the cooking process.

> **RECOMMENDED CHILLIES:** Ring of Fire, Cherry Bomb, Zanzibar chillies for the stew. Fatali, Antillais Caribbean or Scotch Bonnet to sprinkle.

)))) Spanish Tortilla with Roasted Piquillo Peppers

Here are simple ingredients, carefully cooked with a little chilli twist. It really is hard to go wrong with a tortilla. Eaten hot or cold, for lunch, supper or even as a main meal, it is always welcome. It is worth remembering that this is not anything like a French omelette; it requires comparably long and gentle cooking. Like the Italian frittata it is, however, always worth the wait.

50 ml/3 tablespoons olive oil

2 large white onions, thinly sliced

2 large potatoes, peeled and thinly sliced

4 roasted Piquillo peppers (see 'My Tip'), roughly chopped

6 eggs

sea salt and freshly ground black pepper

green salad, to serve

large, heavy-based, lidded frying pan (about 28 cm/11 in.) plus a plate slightly larger than the frying pan

Serves 6 as a starter, 4 as a light meal or 2 as a generous main

Heat half the oil in the large, heavy-based frying pan, add the onions and potatoes and toss to coat. Season well and add the Piquillo peppers. Turn down the heat and cover with a lid. Cook until the potatoes and onions are soft and translucent, about 20 minutes. Turn regularly to prevent too much browning. Once they are softened, remove them from the oil with a slotted spoon and set aside.

Lightly whisk the eggs in a large mixing bowl and add the onions and potatoes (they should still be hot so that the cooking process of the eggs begins as soon as they are mixed together). Season with salt and pepper. Add the rest of the oil to the pan and return to medium heat. Pour the egg mixture into the hot pan – it should fill it by about two-thirds. Turn the heat down to its lowest setting and cook for 20–25 minutes until there is very little liquid on the surface.

Take the plate that is slightly larger than the frying pan and place it upside down over the frying pan. Invert the plate and pan, tipping the tortilla out onto the plate. Put the pan back on the heat and gently slide the tortilla back into it. The cooked side is now facing upward and the uncooked side will now be on the heat. Cook for a further 2–3 minutes. Turn off the heat and let settle. (If you don't feel up to flipping the tortilla over, you can grill/broil the top for 2–3 minutes.)

Turn the tortilla out onto a clean plate and slice to serve. I must admit to loving a splash of hot sauce with mine. And it's great with a green salad and a glass of good Spanish Rioja.

MY TIP: Fresh Piquillo peppers come from northern Spain and are harvested in September and December. You can roast them (preferably over an open fire or barbecue) and peel them for this recipe. Ready-roasted peppers are available from good Spanish importers, peeled and packed into delicious Spanish olive oil.

> **RECOMMENDED CHILLIES:** Piquillo are obviously perfect for this although, at a push, you could substitute any hot sweet Piquanté peppers you can find at your local store.

Vegetable Chilli Roast with Mushroom & Tarragon Gravy

If you are ever at a loose end in Newcastle-upon-Tyne and you have grown tired of the endless stag and hen groups that seem to wander the streets every weekend, then I can't recommend highly enough a brisk walk over to Ouseburn and Stepney Bank. It is a great creative and artistic centre for the city and has one of the best music pubs you will ever visit; The Cluny! I had a fantastic vegetarian roast there which changed my opinion of this much maligned dish. This is our own version, ideal for a 'chilli' Sunday lunch.

1 tablespoon olive oil

knob of butter

1 red onion, finely chopped

2 garlic cloves, finely chopped

1–2 Jalapeño chillies, deseeded and finely diced

½ red sweet/bell pepper, deseeded and diced

1 small courgette/zucchini, finely chopped

6 small mushrooms, chopped

125 g/1 cup mixed shelled nuts, chopped

130 g/1⅓ cups fresh breadcrumbs

100 g/3½ oz. feta cheese, crumbled

100 g/3½ oz. cheddar, grated

sea salt and freshly ground black pepper

Mushroom & tarragon gravy

knob of butter

1 small red onion, finely chopped

6 small mushrooms, finely chopped

1 teaspoon dried tarragon

125 ml/½ cup good red wine

1 teaspoon tomato purée/paste

150 ml/⅔ cup boiling water

1 teaspoon vegetable bouillon powder

very small handful of fresh flat leaf parsley, finely chopped

baking dish, about 1.5-litre/6-cup capacity

Serves 4

Preheat the oven to 200°C (400°F) Gas 6.

Heat the oil and most of the butter in a frying pan over medium heat and gently fry the onion for 1–2 minutes, then add the garlic. Fry until the onion starts to soften. Add the chillies, sweet/bell pepper, courgette/zucchini and mushrooms and cook for 5 minutes, stirring regularly. Remove from the heat. In a large bowl, combine the cooked mixture with the nuts, breadcrumbs and the cheeses. Mix really well.

Lightly grease the baking dish with the rest of the butter. Spoon the mixture into the dish and press firmly down to ensure the roast is tightly packed into the dish with no large air pockets. Cover the top of the mixture with baking parchment. Roast in the preheated oven for 35–40 minutes and remove the paper for the last 5 minutes to brown the surface.

Once cooked, remove from the oven and let rest for a few minutes before serving; this will allow it to firm up if it is a little soft when it is first removed from the oven.

Meanwhile, to make the mushroom & tarragon gravy, melt the butter in a frying pan and fry the onion for 2 minutes. Add the mushrooms and fry gently until soft. Season with a little salt and add the tarragon. Turn up the heat and add the wine. Bubble to reduce by about half; this will evaporate the alcohol leaving the intensified wine flavour.

Add the tomato purée/paste, boiling water and vegetable bouillon powder, mix and simmer over reduced heat for about 5 minutes, then add more boiling water if required. Pour the gravy into a small bowl and blend with a hand blender until smooth. Return to the pan, reheat and season to taste. Add more boiling water if required, throw in the parsley and mix through. Keep warm until required. Serve with roast or mashed potatoes, roast parsnips, peas and broccoli.

RECOMMENDED CHILLIES: Cherry Bomb, red Jalapeño or any other supermarket red.

Chilli Veggie Burger with Sun-dried Tomatoes & Spicy Red Onion Relish

Everybody likes good vegetarian food! The problem is that it often seems to have been thrown together as something of an ill-considered afterthought. These burgers put all that right. They are deliciously savoury and just spicy enough, with wonderful sweet hints from the sun-dried tomatoes. The polenta/cornmeal gives the burger a lovely hint of crunch.

1 sweet potato, peeled and chopped into 2.5-cm/1-inch cubes

3 garlic cloves, skins on

olive oil, for drizzling

40 g/3 tablespoons Puy lentils (or other green lentils)

1 teaspoon vegetable bouillon powder

60 g/½ cup fresh wholemeal/whole-wheat breadcrumbs

1 carrot, grated

6–8 sun-dried tomatoes, finely chopped

1 medium–hot red chilli, deseeded and finely chopped

1 teaspoon balsamic vinegar

1 teaspoon dried oregano

1 teaspoon dark soy sauce

1 teaspoon Cajun spice blend

1 small egg, lightly beaten

1 tablespoon plain/all-purpose flour

1 tablespoon polenta/cornmeal

celery salt and freshly ground black pepper

8 burger buns, warmed, to serve

rocket/arugula leaves, to serve

Spicy Red Onion Relish (page 121), to serve

Makes 8 burgers

Preheat the oven to 160°C (325°F) Gas 3.

Put the sweet potato in a roasting dish with the garlic and drizzle liberally with olive oil. Roast in the preheated oven for about 40 minutes, or until the potato is soft and just beginning to colour around the edges. Remove from the oven and let cool slightly.

Meanwhile, place the lentils in a pan of cold water with the vegetable bouillon, bring to the boil, then reduce the heat to a simmer and cook for 20–25 minutes until tender. Once the lentils are ready, drain them and place in a large mixing bowl. To the lentils, add the breadcrumbs, carrot, sun-dried tomatoes, chilli, vinegar, oregano, soy sauce and Cajun spice blend.

Add the cooled sweet potato. Make sure the garlic is cool too, then squeeze it out from its skin into the mix too. Using your hands, thoroughly combine all the ingredients together. Season with celery salt and pepper. Add the egg to the mix to bind everything together – again it is easiest to use your hands to do this. If the burger mix is too wet, add another handful of breadcrumbs to it.

Mix the flour and polenta/cornmeal together in a wide dish or shallow bowl. Form the burger mix into 8 equal balls, roll in the flour and polenta mix and shape the ball into a flattened burger shape. Cover with clingfilm/plastic wrap until ready to cook.

Heat a little olive oil in a frying pan and fry the burgers over medium heat for about 5 minutes each side, turning frequently. Serve in warm buns with rocket/arugula leaves and spicy red onion relish.

RECOMMENDED CHILLIES: Jalapeño, Serrano or Cherry Bomb.

side dishes

Chilli-brushed Roast Potatoes with Garlic & Rosemary

New Mexico Potato Salad

Cajun-spiced, Souffléd Baked Potatoes

Roast Tomatoes with Chilli, Bay & Thyme

Beck's Tarka Dhal

Green Chilli Bhajis

Patatas Bravas, or Fierce Potatoes

Devilled Bubble & Squeak

Potato, Celeriac & Wild Garlic Gratin

)))) New Mexico Potato Salad (left)

A simple, tasty and inventive way of using the first potatoes of the new season, this is a great accompaniment to anything from the barbecue/grill.

6 medium waxy potatoes, eg Ratte or Charlotte, scrubbed

1 tablespoon olive oil

1 tablespoon freshly squeezed lemon juice

4 large free-range eggs

4 large, mild green chillies, roughly chopped

5 large spring onions/scallions, chopped

200 g/a scant cup mayonnaise

sea salt and freshly ground black pepper

Serves 4–6

Put the potatoes in a large saucepan of lightly salted boiling water, cover and bring back to the boil. Cook for 25–30 minutes until cooked but still firm. Drain and add the oil and lemon juice. Replace the lid and give them a good shake. Cool to room temperature with the lid on.

Boil the eggs in a small pan of salted water for 10 minutes. Remove from the heat and run the eggs under cold water. Shell them and let cool, then cut into medium-sized pieces. Cube the potatoes and put in a large bowl with the chillies, spring onions/scallions and mayonnaise. Mix well. Add the eggs and stir through very gently. Season to taste.

> RECOMMENDED CHILLIES: Sante Fe, Hungarian Hot Wax.

)))) Chilli-brushed Roast Potatoes with Garlic & Rosemary

These potatoes are a spicy, herby twist on the classic Sunday lunch favourite. Brilliant with any sort of roast, but particularly with Stracotto di Manzo (page 55).

12 medium potatoes (about 1.75 kg/3¾ lbs.), cut in half

8 tablespoons olive oil

3 garlic cloves, skin on

sprig of fresh rosemary

25 g/2 tablespoons butter

¼ teaspoon dried chilli/red pepper flakes

pinch of dried Chipotle (crushed or ground)

sea salt and freshly ground black pepper

Serves 4–6

Preheat the oven to 200°C (400°F) Gas 6.

Put the potatoes in a large saucepan of lightly salted boiling water, cover and bring back to the boil. Turn down the heat and cook for 5 minutes. Drain, return the potatoes to the pan, replace the lid and shake to fluff up the edges. Put 7 tablespoons of the oil in a roasting dish and preheat for 3–4 minutes. Season the potatoes. Add them, with the garlic and rosemary, to the hot oil in the dish. Turn a few times to coat and return to the oven. Heat the remaining oil and the butter in a pan over low heat. Add the dried chilli/pepper flakes and Chipotle and infuse for 5 minutes. Remove the potatoes from the oven, brush with the chilli infusion and roast for 40 minutes, brushing again 2–3 times during cooking. Drain on kitchen paper/paper towels.

> RECOMMENDED CHILLIES: Using Chipotle gives a mildly smoky flavour that works brilliantly with the rosemary and garlic.

))))) Cajun-spiced, Souffléd Baked Potatoes

There are times (not often, thankfully), when we really can't work out what we want to eat. At this time the wonderful baked potato nearly always saves the day. Here is our favourite way of embellishing this humble dish. The possible variations are endless: with the addition of a leafy green salad it is quite easy to turn it into an entire meal or you can keep it simple and serve as an intriguing accompaniment for your main meal.

2 large baking potatoes, scrubbed

large knob of butter

1 big teaspoon Dijon mustard

2 teaspoons Cajun spice blend

2 spring onions/scallions, chopped

1 mild green chilli, deseeded and chopped

100 g/1 cup grated mature/sharp cheddar, plus extra for sprinkling

1 egg, lightly beaten

sea salt and freshly ground black pepper

Serves 2

Preheat the oven to 200°C (400°F) Gas 6.

Pierce the potato skins several times with a fork, then place the potatoes directly on a shelf in the preheated oven. Bake until the flesh is soft enough to scrape out, and the skins are crispy enough to retain their shape – about 50–70 minutes, depending on the size of the potatoes. Leave the oven on.

Once the potatoes are soft, let them cool slightly until they are cool enough to handle. Cut them in half lengthways and carefully spoon the insides into a large bowl. Mash the potato until it is fairly lump-free, then add the butter, mustard, Cajun spice blend, spring onions/scallions, chilli and cheese. (Reserve a couple of pieces of chilli to decorate the tops of the potatoes if you like.) Stir together until well mixed. Check the seasoning – the Cajun spice blend will contain a fair amount of salt, so do taste it before you add too much more. When you are satisfied that the seasoning is right, quickly mix the beaten egg through the mashed potato mixture and then spoon the mixture back into the skins.

Sprinkle some extra grated cheese over the filled potatoes and top with the reserved chilli pieces, if using. Place the potatoes onto a small baking dish and return to the oven for a further 15–20 minutes or until the cheese starts to brown. The egg will cause the potatoes to rise slightly in a sort of scaled-down soufflé effect, giving them an unexpected lightness.

Serve with a tasty mixed salad and simple piece of grilled fish or chicken.

MY TIP: For a tempting and easy supper, add a can of tuna to the potatoes when you mix in the other ingredients.

)))) Roast Tomatoes with Chilli, Bay & Thyme

I first had this dish at a farmhouse high up in the Crete Senesi region of Tuscany. It was late May and, although warm, heavy intermittent showers accentuated the fantastic smell of spring on the breeze. It was a magical place. Since then this simple flavour most signifies to me that summer has arrived. Sit down with a modest glass of chilled wine and enjoy this straight from the roasting dish with torn, crusty fresh bread – you can almost hear the sheep bells echoing across the valley! This recipe can also be used as a delicious topping for bruschetta or can be blended down to make a delicious roast tomato sauce for homemade pizza or pasta.

8 tablespoons extra virgin olive oil (preferably Tuscan)

1 kg/2¼ lbs. very ripe tomatoes (large vine tomatoes work best)

4 garlic cloves, bruised and skin on

3 fresh bay leaves

2 sprigs of fresh thyme

2 teaspoons balsamic vinegar

½ hot red chilli, finely chopped

celery salt and freshly ground black pepper

small bunch of your favourite fresh herb, eg rosemary or oregano, chopped

large, heavy ceramic baking dish

Serves 4–6

Preheat the oven to 160°C (325°F) Gas 3.

Use 1 tablespoon of the oil to lightly grease the large, heavy ceramic baking dish. Cut the tomatoes in half vertically from the stem down. Arrange them snugly in the baking dish, cut side up.

Push the garlic cloves and bay leaves in between the tomatoes, add the thyme and pour the remaining oil evenly over the tomatoes, making sure that each one is well coated. Sprinkle the vinegar over the top.

Scatter the chilli evenly across the tomatoes and season the entire dish generously with celery salt and black pepper. Finally, toss your chosen chopped herbs over everything.

Roast in the preheated oven for about 2 hours. When cooked, the tomatoes will be lightly browned on top and oozing rich juices. If it looks like they're burning, turn the oven temperature down slightly. Remove from the oven and while still hot, gently squeeze each tomato with the back of a fork to release more of the juice. Be careful – they tend to spray juice!

Let cool slightly. This will encourage the caramelized sugar in the roasted tomatoes to thicken, combining with the herbs, oil and vinegar to make a wonderful sauce. They can be served warm or cold with fresh crusty bread.

MY TIPS: To bruise garlic, lay it on a level surface and put the flat side of a chef's knife on top of it. Bump the flat part of the blade with your palm to crack open the clove. Its juices will seep out while cooking.

If you are unable to get tomatoes that are really ripe, a delicate sprinkling of sugar will encourage them to caramelize during cooking.

RECOMMENDED CHILLIES: Italian Peperoncino Piccante or Serrano is ideal if available.

 # Beck's Tarka Dhal

This is fantastic as a tasty, nourishing meal just served with 'parathas' (Indian flatbreads) or other flatbread, but is equally brilliant served as an accompaniment to a curry. I don't really like the term 'fusion food', but I suppose the addition of Italian passata in this dhal recipe is just that – it gives a rich tomatoey flavour to the dhal and intensifies the wonderful colour of the red lentils. Even our one-year-old loves it – her mother came up with it for her... spoilt!

25 g/2 tablespoons butter

2 tablespoons sunflower oil

1 white onion, thinly sliced

1 teaspoon yellow mustard seeds

½ teaspoon fenugreek seeds

½ teaspoon ground ginger

3 garlic cloves, finely chopped

125 g/⅔ cup red split lentils

350 g/1½ cups creamed tomatoes or passata (Italian strained tomatoes)

freshly squeezed juice of 1 lemon

generous handful of fresh coriander/cilantro, finely chopped

1 teaspoon garam masala

½ teaspoon mild, medium or hot chilli powder/ground red chile (depending on taste)

sea salt and freshly ground black pepper

Serves 4 as a side dish or 2 as a main

In a heavy-based shallow saucepan (we actually use a wok for this!), melt half the butter with half the oil. Add the onion and cook over fairly high heat for about 3 minutes, until it is starting to soften and turn very slightly brown around the edges.

Add the mustard seeds, cover, and wait until you hear them start to pop. Remove the lid and add the fenugreek, ginger and garlic and give everything a good stir for about 30 seconds.

Thoroughly rinse the lentils, then add with the creamed tomatoes and 450 ml/2 cups water to the pan and gently bring to the boil. Simmer, uncovered, for about 15 minutes.

Add the lemon juice and coriander/cilantro and cook for about 5–10 minutes over low heat until the dhal begins to reduce and absorb any excess liquid. The dhal should be almost porridge-like in consistency, ie thick enough that you can scoop it up with a *paratha*! Season with salt and pepper to taste.

Meanwhile, in a separate pan, heat the remaining butter and oil, add the garam masala and chilli powder/ground red chile and fry for 30 seconds before drizzling all over the dhal.

MY TIP: Add some pep to the chilli-garam masala oil by putting ½ teaspoon dried chilli/red pepper flakes in with ¼ teaspoon chilli powder/ground red chile and 1 teaspoon garam masala.

)))) Green Chilli Bhajis

These exotic and tasty bhajis are wonderfully adaptable. I have never been a fan of making food that is absurdly hot but I have, on occasion, been tempted to do so with these! Substituting the mild green chillies for deseeded and shredded green Habaneros makes a bhaji that will live long in anyone's memory – despite its delicious flavour, the intense heat can limit table conversation a little!

500 ml/2 cups sunflower oil

4 tablespoons coriander seeds

4 tablespoons nigella (black onion) seeds

4 tablespoons yellow mustard seeds

4 tablespoons fenugreek seeds

1 tablespoon fennel seeds

½ teaspoon whole cloves

1 large onion, finely diced

3–4 garlic cloves, finely chopped

5-cm/2-inch piece of fresh ginger, peeled and finely chopped

100 g/3½ oz. mild green chillies, finely chopped

60 g/¼ cup plain whole yogurt

grated zest and freshly squeezed juice of 2 limes

250 g/2 cups gram (chickpea) flour

250 g/2 cups cornflour/cornstarch

3 tablespoons hot curry powder (either Madras or Malay-style citrusy)

sea salt and freshly ground black pepper

Caramelized lime, mint & yogurt dip

1 teaspoon groundnut oil

1 lime, quartered, plus extra lime zest, to garnish

300 g/1¼ cups plain yogurt

a few fresh mint leaves

cooking thermometer (optional)

Makes about 16

To make the caramelized lime, mint & yogurt dip, heat the oil in a frying pan over medium heat. Add the lime quarters and fry each cut side until the surface begins to develop a strong colour. It can be useful to push the lime onto the hot surface of the pan to speed this process – this will force out a little more of the juice, aiding the caramelization. Mix the yogurt and a pinch of black pepper in a small bowl. Squeeze the juice from the caramelized limes into the bowl. Take half the mint leaves and roughly tear them, then add to the bowl, too. Stir, then garnish with the rest of the lime leaves and a little lime zest. Set aside.

Put the sunflower oil in a large saucepan. Heat until it reaches 190°C (375°F) on a cooking thermometer. If you don't have a cooking thermometer, the oil is ready when a 2.5-cm/1-inch cube of white bread dropped into it browns in less than 60 seconds.

Meanwhile, toast all the seeds and the cloves in a hot, dry frying pan over medium heat until the seeds start to pop. Grind them using a pestle and mortar. Put the ground spices along with all the remaining ingredients in a mixing bowl and mix. Gradually add 250 ml/1 cup water until the final mixture is firm but will drop from a spoon.

Place about 3 separate tablespoonfuls of the bhaji mix in the hot oil and fry for about 8 minutes, or until golden brown. Remove the bhajis from the pan using a slotted spoon and let drain on kitchen paper/paper towels before serving. Continue to cook the remaining bhajis in batches and keep the already cooked bhajis warm until needed.

Serve with the caramelized lime, mint & yogurt dip.

> **MY TIP:** For a fiery option, use Indian Green Finger, green Bird's Eye or even green Habanero.

)))) Patatas Bravas, or Fierce Potatoes

Known worldwide as a great tapas dish, this classic Spanish recipe takes all the flavours of rural Spain and combines them to wonderful effect. As with the majority of simple dishes, the success of this recipe is defined by the quality of the ingredients that go into it. Fresh potatoes and garlic, ripe tomatoes and chilli and good-quality olive oil make this a delight to make as well as eat!

400 g/14 oz. new waxy potatoes, eg Ratte or Pink Fir Apple, scrubbed

1 tablespoon olive oil

2 garlic cloves, crushed

1 hot red chilli, deseeded and finely chopped

2–3 large, ripe tomatoes, roughly chopped

pinch of sweet smoked paprika (pimentón dulce)

½ teaspoon paprika

pinch of saffron strands

1 teaspoon dried wild oregano

2 tablespoons olive oil (or 1 olive oil and 1 chilli oil)

sea salt flakes and freshly ground black pepper

Serves 4 as a side or tapas dish

Cut the potatoes into 2-cm/¾-inch pieces. Put them in a large saucepan of lightly salted boiling water, cover and bring back to the boil. Cook until they are cooked through but still firm. Drain and pat dry with kitchen paper/paper towels.

Put the 1 tablespoon oil in a small frying pan over medium heat and fry the garlic and chilli for about 1 minute. Add the tomatoes and cook for a further 2 minutes. Add both types of paprika, the saffron and oregano. Stir and cook for a further 5–10 minutes until the flavours have fully mingled and the tomatoes have softened. Remove from the heat and cover.

Put the 2 tablespoons oil in a large frying pan over medium–high heat and fry the now-dry cubes of potato until golden brown and crispy. Season these with salt and pepper and serve topped with the spicy tomato sauce.

MY TIP: Frying the potatoes in the Smoked Chilli & Rosemary Oil (page 130) adds a fantastic depth of flavour to this dish, infusing the potato cubes with a herby, garlicky, slightly smoky flavour.

> **RECOMMENDED CHILLIES:** Red Bird's Eye.

)))) Devilled Bubble & Squeak

Part of being a good cook is being able to make something inviting from the ingredients you have to hand. English 'bubble and squeak' in any of its variations helps you do that wonderfully well. It is a true comfort food. The results are tasty and filling and it essentially uses bits and pieces that may otherwise have been thrown away, although traditionally it is made with leftover cabbage and potato. My Dad used to love it; having grown up during the Second World War it was a dish that, for him, beautifully summed up the old adage 'waste not, want not' (even if we did occasionally make it from scratch!)

25g/2 tablespoons butter

1 large onion, finely chopped

1 garlic clove, crushed (optional)

1 large cooked potato (about 250 g/8½ oz.), cubed or roughly mashed

150 g/5 oz. cooked Brussels sprouts, finely chopped

50 g/½ cup cooked, shredded cabbage or other leafy green vegetable

handful of frozen peas (optional)

1 tablespoon hot chilli sauce (your favourite!)

1 tablespoon Worcestershire sauce

sea salt and freshly ground black pepper

Serves 2

Melt the butter in a frying pan over medium heat and gently fry the onion for 2–3 minutes. Increase the heat slightly and add the garlic and potato. Fry for another 2 minutes, or until the onion and garlic have softened.

Add the Brussels sprouts, cabbage, peas, if using, chilli sauce and Worcestershire sauce. Continue cooking for a further 8–10 minutes, turning everything 2 or 3 times to ensure it is heating through but allowing the potato to brown. Season with salt and pepper.

To serve, we suggest serving the bubble and squeak with a fried egg on top for a hearty breakfast. You might also want to splash some extra chilli sauce on top!

MY TIP: This recipe can be altered to include whatever leftover vegetables you have to hand. As a general rule, though, it needs to have potato in some form and some kind of green, leafy veg. Apart from that, the only rule is that there are none.

RECOMMENDED CHILLIES: Ring of Fire for heat, or Santa Fe (or Hungarian Hot Wax) for a milder version.

)))) Potato, Celeriac & Wild Garlic Gratin

Seasonal cooking is great, especially when you just never see the ingredient again until the same time next year. Wild garlic (also known as ramsons or ramps) – particularly the leaves – is such a spring treat. For a few weeks each spring the banks and roadsides are covered with these fantastically aromatic plants. The leaves make a wonderful addition to any pesto (see page 133) and as with this dish, add a bit of fresh garlicky oomph to any potato recipe.

25 g/2 tablespoons butter

3–4 shallots, finely chopped

1 leek, finely chopped

2 garlic cloves, crushed

1 teaspoon ground Ancho or other dried chilli

a few wild garlic leaves or spinach leaves, roughly chopped

150 ml/⅔ cup milk

100 ml/a scant ½ cup double/heavy cream

1 green chilli, deseeded and finely chopped

3 large potatoes (about 600 g/ 1 lb. 4 oz.) peeled and thinly sliced

150 g/5 oz. celeriac, peeled and thinly sliced

about 50 g/½ cup grated Parmesan

olive oil, for drizzling

sea salt and freshly ground black pepper

rocket/arugula, watercress and spinach salad, to serve

Chilli Pickled Onions (see page 49)

ovenproof dish, lightly greased

Serves 4

Preheat the oven to 180°C (350°F) Gas 4.

Melt the butter in a frying pan and gently fry the shallots, leek and garlic with the ground Ancho for about 10 minutes, or until soft. Add the wild garlic leaves or spinach and allow to wilt over gentle heat.

In a separate pan, heat the milk, cream and chilli over low heat for about 10 minutes to infuse the milk with the chilli flavour.

Put the potato and celeriac slices into a large bowl. Add the cooked leek mixture and mix well, ensuring everything is evenly coated. Layer the slices in the prepared ovenproof dish, seasoning well between each layer. Pour the infused milk mixture over the vegetables, ensuring that the shredded chilli is evenly distributed. Sprinkle the Parmesan over the top and season with a little extra salt and pepper. Cover the dish with foil and bake in the preheated oven for about 1 hour.

Remove the foil and drizzle a little olive oil evenly over the gratin. Put back in the oven, uncovered, and cook for about 15 minutes, or until the potatoes are nicely golden on the top.

Serve with a rocket/arugula, watercress and spinach salad and a few chilli pickled onions.

MY TIP: If you wish to make the garlic flavour more pronounced, add a few more wild garlic leaves. If you can't find any wild garlic leaves, or they are out of season, spinach leaves will work well for colour.

> **RECOMMENDED CHILLIES:** Mild–medium green chilli.

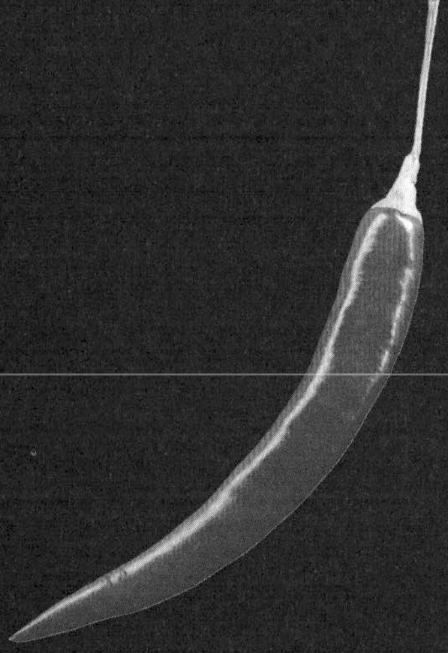

sauces, salsas & marinades

Roast Garlic & Chipotle Mayo

Quick Chilli Lime Mayo

Fresh Aïoli

Salsa Cruda

Green Pepper, Tomato & Habanero Chilli Salsa

Habanero Marmalade

Spicy Red Onion Relish

The Ultimate Arrabbiata Pasta Sauce

Tuna & Peas in a Creamy Cajun-seasoned Sauce

The Perfect Puttanesca Pasta Sauce

Jamaican Jerk Marinade

Olio di Peperoncino Piccante, or Proper Chilli Pizza Oil

Smoked Chilli & Rosemary Oil

Nuoc Cham, or Vietnamese-style Dipping Sauce

Wild Garlic & Chilli Pesto

Dan's Traditional Texas Chilli Powder

Dukkah

Provençal Herb Blend

)))) Roast Garlic & Chipotle Mayo

This lovely mayonnaise is really big on flavour. It's just right for alternative egg mayonnaise sandwiches or an amazing potato salad.

2 large garlic cloves, skin on

4 tablespoons mayonnaise

½ teaspoon crushed Chipotle chilli

Makes 4 tablespoons

Preheat the oven to 180°C (350°F) Gas 4.

Roast the garlic on a baking sheet in the preheated oven for 20 minutes until soft but not burnt. Remove from the oven and let cool for 10 minutes. Squeeze the garlic from its skin into a small bowl. Gently mash with a fork. Add the mayonnaise and Chipotle and stir until evenly mixed. Cover and refrigerate for 2–3 hours to let the Chipotle rehydrate a little in the mayonnaise. Stir occasionally while it's chilling.

)))) Quick Chilli Lime Mayo

This is a hot and fruity mayonnaise that literally takes seconds to make. It's great with any seafood and does wonders for a tuna sandwich!

4 tablespoons mayonnaise

grated zest and freshly squeezed juice of 1 small lime

1 Scotch Bonnet chilli, very finely chopped

Makes 4 tablespoons

Mix the mayonnaise and lime juice in a small bowl. Add the Scotch Bonnet, little by little, until the desired hotness is achieved. Garnish with lime zest.

)))) Fresh Aïoli

This is an all-time classic dip, brilliant with potatoes or anything barbecued/grilled, particularly prawns/shrimp or chicken. This recipe has a wonderful robust garlicky flavour.

2 large egg yolks

4 very fresh garlic cloves, crushed

1 teaspoon Dijon mustard

150 ml/⅔ cup good-quality light olive oil

freshly squeezed juice of ½ lemon

sea salt and freshly ground black pepper

Makes about 200 ml/¾ cup

Beat the eggs yolks in a large bowl with a balloon whisk. Add the garlic and mustard and beat through. While beating the mixture, slowly add the olive oil in a thin, steady stream. When all the oil has been added, the aïoli should have a smooth, velvety appearance. Add the lemon juice, season with salt and pepper and gently stir through. Refrigerate until needed.

 ## Salsa Cruda (right)

Salsa cruda is more commonly known as 'pico de gallo' in Mexican – it means rooster's beak! I love that the onion and chilli are marinated in the lime juice instead of being stirred through the juice at the end – this helps to round the flavour of the onion and, to a lesser extent, the chillies.

1 Serrano chilli
1 Poblano chilli
3 Jalapeño chillies
1 red onion, finely chopped
2 spring onions/scallions, finely chopped
120 ml/½ cup freshly squeezed lime juice
3 tomatoes, roughly chopped
1 avocado, roughly chopped
small handful of fresh coriander/cilantro, chopped
sea salt and freshly ground black pepper

Makes 200–250 g/1–2 cups

Deseed and finely chop all the chillies. Put the chopped chillies, onion, spring onions/scallions, ½ teaspoon salt and the lime juice in a small bowl and mix well. Refrigerate for 1–2 hours.

Drain off the excess liquid from the refrigerated salsa. Add the tomatoes, avocado and coriander/cilantro. Mix well and season to taste.

> **RECOMMENDED CHILLIES:** Serrano, Poblano and Jalapeño are the perfect combination but the blend needs to be 1 smallish hot chilli, 1 larger milder chilli and 3 juicy, fleshy medium chillies if you need to improvise.

Green Pepper, Tomato & Habanero Chilli Salsa

Real salsas are at their best just after they are made. Once you have experienced these feisty, zingy flavours, you will never go back to supermarket salsa! Eat in burritos or with a plate of nachos.

2 green sweet/bell peppers
120 g/4 oz. cucumber
4 plum tomatoes
2 shallots, finely chopped
1 garlic clove, crushed
handful of fresh flat leaf parsley, chopped
1 Habanero or Scotch Bonnet chilli, very finely chopped
grated zest and freshly squeezed juice of 1 lime
4 tablespoons olive oil
2 tablespoons red wine vinegar
sea salt and freshly ground black pepper

Makes 200–250 g/1–2 cups

Peel, deseed and dice the sweet/bell peppers, cucumber and plum tomatoes.

In a large bowl, combine the shallots, peppers, cucumber, tomatoes, garlic and parsley. Add the chilli, mix thoroughly and season with salt and pepper, to taste. Put the lime zest and juice, oil and vinegar into a small bowl, whisk together to make a dressing and add to the salsa. Toss together well and serve as soon as possible.

> **RECOMMENDED CHILLIES:** Chocolate Habanero, Orange Habanero, Fatali, Scotch Bonnet – this is a salsa for the stout-hearted!

)))) Habanero Marmalade (left)

This fiery marmalade can be used to really wake up your breakfast toast. It is hot and fresh and zesty all at the same time. It also makes an unusual but welcome addition to any cheese board.

750 g/1½ lbs. (about 2) slightly under-ripe grapefruits

500 g/1 lb. (about 3) slightly under-ripe limes

about 1.8 litres/2 quarts water

100 g/3½ oz. Habanero chillies, deseeded

2.5 kg/5½ lbs. granulated sugar

100 ml/½ cup freshly squeezed lemon juice

piece of muslin/cheesecloth

kitchen twine

several jam jars, sterilized (see page 4)

Makes about 3.5 kg/7½ lbs.

Peel the grapefruits and cut the peel into thick shreds. Do the same with the limes (if they're too difficult to peel, dice the whole lime as finely as possible and remove and set aside the seeds). Remove and set aside the seeds from the grapefruit. Squeeze the juice into a bowl and roughly chop the remaining pulp. Put the lime and grapefruit pulp, juice, and peel in a large saucepan with the water. Put all the seeds in a piece of muslin/cheesecloth and tie with kitchen twine. Add to the pan. Bring to the boil, reduce the heat and gently simmer, uncovered, for 1½–1¾ hours. Remove the bag and squeeze any juice into the pan.

To a small bowl, add 150 ml/⅔ cup of the cooking liquid and the chillies. Blend to a smooth purée. Transfer back to the pan and stir. Add the sugar and lemon juice. Bring back to the boil and boil hard for 15–20 minutes. To see if the marmalade has reached setting point, drip a little onto a plate and chill. If it forms a skin, it is ready. If not, return to the heat and test again in 10 minutes. Fill the sterilized jars and seal.

)))) Spicy Red Onion Relish

I love tomato ketchup; nothing else evokes such wonderful memories of childhood barbecues. However, if you are going to cook perfect burgers, they deserve this perfect red onion relish!

½ teaspoon crushed Chipotle or other dried chilli

2 tablespoons hot water

3 tablespoons balsamic vinegar

2 tablespoons olive oil

2 red onions, thinly sliced

1 tablespoon chilli jam/pepper jelly

2 tomatoes, skinned (see page 122) and chopped

squeeze of lemon juice

small bunch of fresh coriander/cilantro, chopped

sea salt and freshly ground black pepper

Makes 200–250 g/1–2 cups

Soak the Chipotle in the hot water for 20 minutes.

Discard the water and add the chillies to the vinegar. Let stand for a further 10 minutes.

Heat the oil in a frying pan over low heat and gently fry the onions for about 20 minutes, or until softened, stirring regularly. Add the vinegar with the chillies. Toss the mixture to coat the onions and continue to cook until the vinegar has evaporated.

Add the chilli jam/pepper jelly, stir through and cook for a further minute. Add the tomatoes and heat through again. Season with a little salt and pepper. Stir in the lemon juice and fresh coriander/cilantro before serving.

//// The Ultimate Arrabbiata Pasta Sauce

In late autumn 2001, I found myself staying with a friend in a hilltop village just outside Volterra, in Tuscany. At this time I was a landscape photographer and was producing a series of images of the surrounding countryside. I spent most of the day walking and carrying equipment; by evening I was starving. My friend was a fantastic cook and made me 'all'arrabbiata' on several occasions. It was the most delicious thing I had ever eaten and I was determined to learn how to make it for myself. This is the end result and I still love eating it to this day!

500 g/1 generous lb. ripe plum tomatoes

4 tablespoons olive oil

2 garlic cloves, bruised and skin on

2 tablespoons Italian red wine

1 red chilli, cut lengthways and deseeded

sprig of fresh rosemary

1 fresh bay leaf

½ teaspoon dried oregano

8–10 fresh basil leaves, torn, plus extra to serve

sea salt and freshly ground black pepper

penne or spaghetti, to serve

grated Parmesan, to serve

Serves 2

RECOMMENDED CHILLIES:
Peperoncino Piccante or hot Cayenne.

To skin the tomatoes, place them in a small bowl and pour enough boiling water over them to cover. Leave for a few seconds until the tomato skins split, then drain the water, run under cold water until the tomatoes are cool enough to handle and peel off the skins. Quarter the tomatoes and remove the seeds.

Heat the oil in a saucepan over medium heat and fry the garlic cloves for a few seconds, then add the wine. Allow to bubble away for about 30 seconds, then add the chopped tomatoes. Add the chilli, rosemary, bay leaf, dried oregano and ½ teaspoon salt, stir and turn the heat down to low so that the sauce is just gently simmering. Cover with a lid and gently cook for about 40–45 minutes.

While the sauce is cooking, give it an occasional stir and taste to check the heat level of the sauce. Once the required level is reached, you can remove and discard the chilli. Add a splash of water if the sauce is becoming too dry in the pan. Once cooked, stir through the basil leaves.

This sauce is a perfect accompaniment to penne or spaghetti. To serve, toss some cooked pasta in the sauce, making sure it is nicely coated. Serve dressed with a little more olive oil, a good grating of Parmesan, some black pepper and a few more fresh basil leaves.

MY TIPS: It is crucial to use ripe tomatoes for this recipe. If these are not available, use canned chopped tomatoes. Drain the juice before adding to the pan. Canned tomatoes use acetic acid to help preserve them and as such, benefit from a longer cooking time than fresh tomatoes. I would recommend an additional 20–30 minutes of simmering to fully remove the 'canned' taste.

If you like your sauce a little hotter, add some dried chilli/red pepper flakes to the sauce with the herbs.

))) Tuna & Peas in a Creamy Cajun-seasoned Sauce

This is a lovely quick supper with a flavour that belies the simple ingredients. It is now a once-a-week staple at home, as it can generally be pulled together from the barest storecupboard. There are some great variations to try; corn makes a great substitute if you find you have no frozen peas, and we have a particular fondness for adding a teaspoonful of Marmite at the same time as the mustard. But you'll either love that idea or hate it – as the saying goes!

1 teaspoon vegetable bouillon powder

50 g/¼ cup red split lentils

1 tablespoon olive oil

15 g/1 tablespoon butter

½ large onion, very finely chopped

1 garlic clove, crushed

1 tablespoon plain/all-purpose flour

50 ml/3 tablespoons white wine

1 teaspoon Cajun spice blend

100 ml/a scant ½ cup milk

1 teaspoon Dijon mustard

185-g/6-oz. can of tuna, drained

100 g/1 cup frozen peas

sea salt and freshly ground black pepper

pasta or basmati rice, to serve

Serves 2

Bring a small pan of 250 ml/1 cup water to the boil and add the vegetable bouillon. Mix well. Thoroughly rinse the lentils, then add to the pan. Reduce the heat and cook for about 20 minutes, or until soft.

Meanwhile, heat the oil and butter in a frying pan over low heat and gently fry the onion and garlic for about 5 minutes, or until slightly softened but not browning. Add the flour and mix through. Continue to cook gently for about 2–3 minutes.

Add the wine and cook until the liquid has evaporated. Add the lentils, their cooking liquid and the Cajun spice blend and mix thoroughly. Remove the pan from the heat and gradually stir in the milk. Return the pan to the heat and bring to a gentle simmer. Add the mustard and cook for a further 10 minutes, stirring regularly; the sauce should be thickening now. Add the tuna and peas, stir and cook for 2 minutes. Season with salt and pepper to taste.

Serve on a bed of basmati rice or with your favourite pasta.

MY TIPS: There are many great variations to this dish. This is the simplest and designed for a quick, hearty supper that everyone in the family will enjoy. We frequently add freshly chopped chilli to the onion and garlic for a hotter dish; or a small handful of chopped fresh herbs (tarragon and parsley work particularly well).

Try varying the fish you use too; canned mackerel works very well or, for a real change, try a smoked mackerel fillet flaked into the sauce, then served with pasta.

)))) The Perfect Puttanesca Pasta Sauce

If there was only one pasta sauce I had to make and eat for the rest of my life, this would be it; and not just a Puttanesca but specifically this Puttanesca. Its flavours capture the sunshine of southern Italy perfectly. It is robust, salty and very satisfying; quick to make, but with wonderfully well-balanced flavours. It needs to be eaten as soon as it is cooked. Most importantly, it is made to partner a full-bodied red wine and is best enjoyed with good company!

50 g/1¾ oz. anchovy fillets in brine or olive oil, drained

3 tablespoons extra virgin olive oil

2 garlic cloves, thinly sliced

1 small, hot, red chilli, deseeded and finely chopped

500 g/1 generous lb. plum tomatoes, skinned (see page 122)

50 g/⅓ cup capers

40 g/¼ cup green olives, pitted and chopped

2 tablespoons tomato purée/paste

100 g/⅔ cup black or Kalamata olives, pitted and chopped

sea salt and freshly ground black pepper

spaghetti (preferably bronze), to serve

Serves 2

Rinse the anchovy fillets under cold water for a few moments to desalt or remove excess oil. Pat the fillets dry on some kitchen paper/paper towels. Chop roughly.

Heat the oil in a saucepan and fry the garlic and chilli for about 3–4 minutes. Keep it moving but allow a little browning. Add the anchovies and continue to fry for about 1 minute, or until they begin to break down. Add the chopped tomatoes, capers, green olives and tomato purée/paste. Stir thoroughly. Turn the heat down and allow to gently bubble away, uncovered, for 20 minutes.

Add the black olives and cook for a further 5 minutes. Season only at the end of cooking, as there is a quite a hit of salt from the anchovies and the capers.

Serve with bronze (or regular) spaghetti and a salad of dolcelatte, tomato, basil and herby salad leaves. The sauce should be robust, strong and salty, and is perfect with a bottle of Puglian Primitivo.

MY TIP: This is great for dinner parties, as it is so quick to cook and gives such complex and delicious flavours. Doubling up the ingredients will give 4 generous portions. I find that unlike most Italian pasta sauces, this does not benefit from the addition of Parmesan, but far be it from me to tell you how to serve your meal!

> Recommended Chillies: Peperoncino Piccante or hot Cayenne.

)))) Jamaican Jerk Marinade

This makes a lovely HOT marinade! By a long and exhaustive process of elimination I seem to find myself instinctively mistrusting people who tell me they can't eat spicy food – as far as I have ever seen, it just does you good. This recipe is therefore something of a litmus test when inviting new friends around for dinner. I am not, of course, suggesting that you shouldn't have friends who avoid spicy food, just that it's probably best not to leave them alone with the single malt after dinner!

2 teaspoons ground allspice

1 tablespoon black peppercorns

1 teaspoon grated nutmeg

1 teaspoon ground cinnamon

1 teaspoon sea salt

3 Scotch Bonnet chillies, roughly chopped

10 spring onions/scallions, roughly chopped

½ onion, roughly chopped

4 garlic cloves, sliced

5 cm/2 inches of fresh ginger, peeled and chopped

small bunch of fresh thyme, chopped

4 fresh bay leaves, torn

2 tablespoons molasses

80 ml/⅓ cup freshly squeezed lime juice

80 ml/⅓ cup sunflower oil

1 tablespoon dark rum

Makes about 300 g/1½ cups

Toast the ground allspice in a hot, dry, heavy-based saucepan over medium heat. When it is ready, it will release a strong aroma. Grind the allspice and peppercorns with a pestle and mortar or a spice grinder until they become quite powdery.

Blend all the ingredients together in a food processor or with a hand blender to form a smooth, thick paste. Place in a clean, airtight container and refrigerate. The flavour of the marinade will improve over time and it will keep refrigerated for at least 4 weeks.

This marinade is extremely hot and is great for chicken or pork.

MY TIP: If you do not have molasses to hand, use pure maple syrup or treacle.

> **RECOMMENDED CHILLIES:** Being a Jamaican marinade, I think the flavour of Scotch Bonnet works brilliantly. However, if you cannot lay your hands on these, I would recommend Antillais Caribbean or Trinidad Congo. These Habanero varieties have a fruity aroma perfectly suited to this recipe.

))))) Olio di Peperoncino Piccante, or Proper Chilli Pizza Oil

Good chilli oil relies not only on the quality of the flavouring ingredients but also on the quality of the carrier oil. To get the most from this recipe, try to find a nice extra virgin oil from southern Italy or Tuscany. The 'peppery' characteristics of this oil combine brilliantly with the heat of the dried chillies. Your pizzas will never be the same again…

2 tablespoons dried chilli/red pepper flakes

4–8 whole dried red chillies, depending on size

450 ml/2 cups extra virgin olive oil

500-ml/2-cup bottle with a stopper, cork or screw top, sterilized (see page 4)

Makes 500 ml/2 cups

Put the dried chilli/red pepper flakes and whole chillies in the sterilized bottle. Fill the bottle with olive oil up to 5 cm/2 inches from the top. Secure the top on the bottle and give it a good shake.

Store in a cool, dark place for at least 1 month. Give the bottle a good shake once a week while it is maturing. As the chillies infuse the oil, it will start to show a hint of chilli red. The oil will reach its full heat after about 3 months.

))))) Smoked Chilli & Rosemary Oil

A variation on conventional chilli oils, this has a lovely aroma from the rosemary as well as a creeping smoky warmth from the Chipotles. It's a particularly great oil for salad dressings, simple pasta dishes, pizzas and as a flavouring for roast potatoes. Occasionally it is possible to find smoked Habanero chillies. These are a wonderful variation, making a very hot, fruity and complex oil from a very simple process.

500 ml/2 cups extra virgin olive oil

5 whole smoked dried Chipotle chillies (or any other smoked chilli)

2 large sprigs of fresh rosemary

4 garlic cloves, bruised and skin on

500-ml/2-cup bottle with a stopper, cork or screw top, sterilized (see page 4)

Makes 500 ml/2 cups

Pour the oil into a saucepan and heat gently. Add the chillies, rosemary and garlic. Gently heat until individual bubbles start to rise from the base of the pan through the oil. Reduce the heat to the lowest setting – it is important to maintain a low enough heat so as not to fry the ingredients. Should this be difficult, you can periodically remove the pan from the heat for a few minutes.

After about 40 minutes, sample the oil by drizzling ½ teaspoon onto some fresh bread. Taste – there should be a subtle yet distinct garlic and rosemary flavour followed by a slow growth of chilli heat. If the heat is not pronounced enough, continue to infuse over low heat, regularly testing until the heat meets your requirements.

Transfer the infused oil to the sterilized bottle. (Discard the chillies, rosemary and garlic if you are planning to store the oil for a long time.) Let the oil cool, then seal tightly. The oil is now ready to use.

)))) Nuoc Cham, or Vietnamese-style Dipping Sauce (left)

Vietnamese cuisine is one of the most interesting and diverse in the world. Nuoc Cham and its variations are now perhaps its most universally available sauce and are added as required to virtually any savoury dish. It is particularly good when drizzled over rice dishes or as a dip for vegetable tempura. It's also an essential ingredient in our Thai-spiced Rare Beef & Warm Rice Noodle Salad (page 30).

1 small lime

3 garlic cloves, crushed

2 small hot green chillies, deseeded and finely chopped

4 teaspoons unrefined golden caster sugar or raw cane sugar

60 ml/¼ cup Vietnamese-style fish sauce

Makes about 150 ml/²⁄₃ cup

RECOMMENDED CHILLIES:
Green Thai, green Finger or small Serrano.

Squeeze the juice from the lime into a small bowl and set aside. Scrape the pulp from the lime and grind it, along with the garlic and chillies, with a pestle and mortar to form a paste. If you find it difficult to get a paste, the ingredients could be briefly pulsed in a food processor. Add 75 ml/⅓ cup water and the sugar to the bowl of lime juice and stir until the sugar has dissolved. Scrape the chilli paste into the bowl, add the fish sauce and mix well.

MY TIPS: Add the finely chopped chillies to the bowl at the end if you prefer not to grind them into the Nuoc Cham.

Vietnamese fish sauce is lighter in style than traditional Nam Pla (Thai fish sauce). If you are unable to source this, Thai-style fish sauce still works well but you may wish to reduce the quantity slightly or add to taste.

)))) Wild Garlic & Chilli Pesto

I frequently make fresh pesto to coat some pasta as a quick supper for the kids – and then, when they eat it, I wish I'd made some for myself. This is a grown-up variation on a classic pesto sauce that introduces a lovely kick of chilli heat and the delicious punch of wild garlic leaves.

75 g/½ cup pine nuts

1 garlic clove, peeled

2 handfuls of wild garlic leaves or fresh purple basil leaves

100 g/1 cup grated Parmesan

4 tablespoons extra virgin olive oil

1 hot green chilli

sea salt and freshly ground black pepper

Serves 2 (as a pasta sauce)

Heat a heavy-based frying pan over medium heat, add the pine nuts and dry fry until they begin to brown. Keep them moving so that they toast evenly. Remove from the pan and set aside to cool a little.

Grind 1 teaspoon salt and the garlic to a paste with a pestle and mortar. Put the paste into a food processor with the pine nuts and remaining ingredients. Pulse until you have a smooth paste. Taste and season with a little more salt and some pepper if required. Add more oil if the paste needs to be looser.

))))) Dan's Traditional Texas Chilli Powder

I used to visit Texas regularly to stay with friends in Dallas and to travel around the wilder areas of the state producing photographs and collecting recipes. This recipe was given to me by an 87-year-old lady from Austin who assured me that it was the most authentic blend in the state. It had been passed down to her and was at least 150 years old. When using a chilli blend like this, it is important to bear in mind that it is really used to flavour and season the dish; fresh chillies would normally be added to increase the heat. It also shows the importance of the magic ingredient in all good chilli powders – cumin.

3 hot red chillies, crushed (ideally de Arbol or if you are really feeling brave, Chiltepin or Piquin)

100 g/⅔ cup dried garlic powder or granules

½ tablespoon sea salt flakes

3 tablespoons dried Mexican oregano

40 g/⅓ cup cumin seeds, toasted and coarsely ground

50 g/⅓ cup crushed dried Nu Mex chilli or other dried red chilli

110 g/1 cup ground Ancho chilli

Makes about 300 g/10 oz.

Combine all the ingredients in a bowl, mixing thoroughly. Pour into an airtight container and store in a cool, dark place. This blend is perfect used in the Texas Marinated Steak recipe (see page 67) and essential to a good chili con carne (see page 56) too!

MY TIP: If you can only get whole dried Ancho chilli, it can be difficult to grind or crush, even in the food processor, because it tends to be rubbery in texture. When using chillies like this, it is a good idea to roast them briefly in the oven to dehydrate them further, which will make it easier for them to break down in the food processor.

Dukkah

This is a real Egyptian treat, ideal to serve as an impromptu nibble at any time of the day. It can be made sometime in advance and stored in an airtight container, preferably in the fridge. It will begin to go a little stale after a few days and lose its fresh, nutty zip, so resist the temptation to make an enormous batch. Serve with strips of warm pitta bread, dipped in best olive oil and then in the dukkah.

100 g/⅔ cup blanched
   hazelnuts
50 g/⅓ cup sesame seeds
2 tablespoons coriander seeds
1 tablespoon cumin seeds
½ teaspoon fennel seeds
½ teaspoon black peppercorns
½ teaspoon medium–hot dried
   chilli/red pepper flakes
½ teaspoon dried mint leaves
2 teaspoons sea salt flakes

Serves 6–8

Toast the hazelnuts in a hot, dry, heavy-based saucepan over medium heat for about 5 minutes, or until they are lightly browned and fragrant. Empty into a clean tea/kitchen towel and rub fairly vigorously to remove any remaining bits of skin. Let cool. Add all the seeds and the peppercorns to the pan and lightly toast until they begin to brown, being careful not to let them burn. Remove from the heat and let cool.

Crush all the ingredients with a pestle and mortar until you get a very coarse powder, or pulse briefly in a food processor.

MY TIP: You can vary this recipe by using blanched almonds or even pistachios in place of the hazelnuts.

Provençal Herb Blend

This blend is wonderfully hardy and fragrant – a lovely reminder of Provençal sunshine in a jar! The Piment d'Espelette chilli used in this blend has been granted an AOC by the French government. This means that it has to be grown in one of the 10 listed villages in the Nive Valley in the foothills of the Pyrenees, otherwise it's not the real thing. Regular hot dried chilli/red pepper flakes may be substituted. Use it to season soups and stews, and as a rub for meat dishes.

2 tablespoons dried thyme
2 tablespoons dried marjoram
2 tablespoons dried savory
1 teaspoon fennel seeds
½ teaspoon dried lavender
   flowers
½ teaspoon dried oregano
½ teaspoon dried Piment
   d'Espelette flakes, or other
   dried chilli/red pepper
   flakes
½ teaspoon dried rosemary

Makes a small pot

Combine all the ingredients in a bowl, mixing thoroughly. Pour into an airtight container and store in a cool, dark place.

sweet things & drinks

Incredibly Easy Chilli Jam Ice Cream

The cooling effect of the dairy ice cream here beautifully balances the heat of the chilli jam/pepper jelly. We make this with our own Trees Can't Dance Chilli Jam, which uses fresh Habanero chillies that give it a lovely fruity heat. You don't have to use ours but be sure to get something with sufficient heat and sweetness, and unless you have a slightly peculiar palate, avoid one containing garlic or onion! Serve the ice cream with pine-nut brittle for ice-cream sophistication extraordinaire!

3 egg yolks

397-g/14-oz. can of sweetened condensed milk

300 ml/1¼ cups double/heavy cream

seeds scraped from ½ vanilla pod/bean or ½ teaspoon vanilla extract

150 g/generous ½ cup good chilli jam/pepper jelly

ice cream machine (optional)

freezerproof lidded container

Serves 4

Put the egg yolks in a large bowl and whisk with an electric handheld whisk (or balloon whisk) for a couple of minutes until they look slightly paler in colour. Set aside.

Put the condensed milk, cream and vanilla in a heavy-based pan over low heat, mix and heat very gently, stirring continuously. Because of the high sugar content of the condensed milk, it can easily stick to the base of the pan if you don't keep it moving. When the mixture is hot, remove the pan from the heat and very slowly pour a steady trickle of it onto the pale egg yolks, whisking continuously until you have added it all. You have to pour the hot liquid very slowly and whisk well otherwise the eggs will scramble in the heat. Now pour everything back into your pan and return to the heat, very gently bringing it up to near boiling point and whisking continuously. Remove from the heat and let cool to room temperature.

Transfer the mixture to an ice cream machine and follow the manufacturer's instructions to achieve a set but not too firm ice cream.

Or if you don't own one of these, just pour it into a freezerproof container with a lid, seal tightly and freeze for a good couple of hours. After an hour or two, remove the container from the freezer and give the mixture a good whisk. This will prevent ice crystals from forming and keep the texture smooth and velvety. Repeat this process a couple more times until the mixture is fairly firm and holding its shape.

Put the chilli jam/pepper jelly in a heatproof bowl over a pan of hot water and heat very gently to make the jam as runny as possible. You don't want the jam to get hot, as this will melt the ice cream, but the idea is to get the jam runny enough that you can swirl it through the ice cream. When the jam runs off the back of a spoon, it is ready. Pour it onto your ice cream and, with a large spoon or spatula, fold it into the mixture, creating a marbled ripple effect. Now cover the ice cream again and return it to the freezer, ideally leaving it overnight. If you are using an ice cream machine, you will probably want to transfer the ice cream to a freezerproof container before you get to the jam stage.

))) Chilli Pecan Brownies

Containing coriander seeds, cardamom, cinnamon, nutmeg and black pepper (amongst other spices), Baharat spice blend is a perfect spicy addition to any dark chocolate dish. The caramelized nuts can also be served on their own as a sweet nibble or to finish a meal with a full-bodied coffee.

Caramelized chilli pecans

2 tablespoons (caster) sugar

100 g/⅔ cup chopped pecans

1 teaspoon hot chilli powder/ ground red chile

a pinch of salt

Brownies

100 g/3½ oz. dark/bittersweet (75% cocoa solids) chocolate, broken into pieces

125 g/1 stick unsalted butter, chopped

250 g/1¼ cups (caster) sugar

3 large eggs, lightly beaten

1 teaspoon vanilla extract

200 g/1⅔ cups plain/ all-purpose flour

2 teaspoons Baharat spice blend (see page 4)

a pinch of salt

23 x 33-cm/9 x 13-inch baking pan, greased and lined with baking parchment

Makes about 12 squares

Preheat the oven to 180°C (350°F) Gas 4.

To make the caramelized chilli pecans, put 50 ml/3 tablespoons water and the sugar in a small frying pan over medium heat and stir with a wooden spatula for 2 minutes. Add the pecans and stir well as the water evaporates. After 3–4 minutes, add the chilli powder/ground chile and salt, stirring all the time and making sure the pecans are evenly coated. Continue stirring for a few minutes longer until all the water has evaporated, the pecans are coated and the pan is dry. Tip the pecans onto a plate or waxed paper to cool.

To make the brownies, melt the chocolate and the butter in a large heavy-based saucepan over low heat. Stir well with a wooden spoon until thoroughly melted and smooth, then let cool for a few minutes. Add the sugar and mix.

Beat the eggs and vanilla into the chocolate mixture in the pan with the wooden spoon until well blended. Sift the flour, Baharat spice blend and salt into the pan and stir until just mixed. Stir in the caramelized pecans.

Pour the batter into the prepared baking pan, spreading it evenly. Bake in the preheated oven for 25–30 minutes until firm to the touch or until a skewer inserted into the middle comes out clean. Let cool in the baking pan on a wire rack, then cut the brownies into squares. They should last for 1 week in an airtight container.

MY TIP: For an interesting plate of nibbles, follow the recipe above for the caramelized chilli pecans, substituting about half for macadamia nuts. Leave the nuts whole instead of chopping. Substitute the teaspoon chilli powder for 2 teaspoons Baharat spice blend. Let cool before serving.

))) Deliciously Boozy Truffles with Ginger & Chilli Praline

When my wife's cousin Sian gave us this ganache recipe years ago, the first ingredient listed was a bottle of good red wine. I wasn't sure how this was going to feature until I saw the words: 'pour yourself a decent-sized glass of wine and take a few good gulps'. If I forget to include this stage in any of the recipes in this book, please feel free to incorporate it where appropriate. This is our absolute favourite truffle recipe: an incredibly punchy brandy core rolled in a deliciously crunchy ginger and chilli praline and encased in a thick layer of dark chocolate. The first thing to hit you is the brandy, then the velvety smoothness of the truffle, leaving you with the gentle warmth of the chilli and ginger.

150 g/5 oz. dark/bittersweet chocolate, broken into pieces

Truffle ganache

225 g/7 oz. milk chocolate, broken into pieces

90 ml/6 tablespoons double/heavy cream

45 ml/3 tablespoons brandy

Praline

30 g/¼ cup unsalted, skinned pistachio nuts, roughly chopped

30 g/¼ cup blanched almonds, roughly chopped

1 teaspoon ground ginger

1 dried chilli, preferably Cayenne, cut as finely as possible

90 g/a scant ½ cup golden caster sugar/raw cane sugar

small, deep lidded container, about 1.5-litre/6-cup capacity

2 large sheets of baking parchment, one greased

cocktail stick/toothpick

Makes about 20

To make the truffle ganache, put the chocolate and cream in a heatproof bowl over a saucepan of gently simmering water. Do not let the base of the bowl touch the water. Stir occasionally and once melted, remove from the heat. Pour the brandy into the bowl but don't mix it! Let cool completely, then mix until smooth. Pour into the lidded container, seal and freeze for at least 3 hours.

To make the praline, preheat the oven to 160°C (325°F) Gas 3. Put the nuts, ginger and dried chilli on a baking sheet, shake to mix and roast in the preheated oven for 8 minutes, or until just colouring. Put 60 ml/¼ cup water and the sugar in a heavy-based pan and gently heat for about 10 minutes, or until the sugar has dissolved – don't stir, just swirl the pan to stop the sugar from sticking to the bottom. Turn up the heat and bring to a bubbling boil. Don't let it burn – you can always return the pan to the heat if it needs a little longer, but if you burn it you will have to start again. Once the caramel starts to turn golden, it is ready. If you dip a spoon into the caramel, it will start to set almost immediately. Add the roasted nuts to the caramel, stir to coat, then turn out onto the greased baking parchment. It will be very sticky but try to spread it with a greased knife. Let cool. If it doesn't start to set to a brittle consistency as it cools, return it to the pan and bring it back up to the boil – it probably just needs a bit longer.

Once set, crush with a pestle and mortar or a wooden spoon into small, rough pieces – they can vary in size. Transfer to a small bowl.

Melt the dark/bittersweet chocolate in a bowl over a saucepan, as above. Let cool slightly. Remove the ganache from the freezer. Scoop out teaspoonfuls, roll into a ball and roll firmly in the crushed praline. Push a cocktail stick/toothpick into the truffle and dip in the melted chocolate to coat. Use a teaspoon to help you cover the truffle evenly. Allow any excess chocolate to drip off, then place onto baking parchment and remove the stick. Let cool before refrigerating to set.

)))) Chilli, Chocolate Chunk & Ginger Cookies

These are ridiculously easy to make, use ingredients that are likely to be sitting in the cupboard waiting for you, and taste delicious... what are you waiting for? Go and make some!

100 g/¾ cup plain/all-purpose flour

½ teaspoon baking powder

½ teaspoon hot chilli powder/ground red chile

50 g/¼ cup golden caster sugar/raw cane sugar

85 g/6 tablespoons butter, slightly softened

½ teaspoon vanilla extract

2 teaspoons milk

100 g/3½ oz. dark/bittersweet chocolate, broken into pieces

3 pieces of stem ginger, chopped into small, chunky slices

1–2 baking sheets, well greased

Makes 8 large cookies

Preheat the oven to 180°C (350°F) Gas 4.

In a large mixing bowl, sift together the flour, baking powder and chilli powder/ground chile. Stir in the sugar. Add the butter, vanilla and milk and using your hands or a wooden spoon, mix together until you have a dough-like consistency. Now add the chocolate and ginger pieces, and again using your hands, combine these ingredients so that they are spread evenly throughout the mixture. Very lightly flour your hands, then divide the dough into 8 and roll into balls. Squash slightly until about 6 cm/2¼ inches in diameter and arrange on a prepared baking sheet. When baking, the cookies relax and spread out quite a lot, so space them well apart. If you find that they're too squashed on one baking sheet, arrange some cookies on a second greased baking sheet.

Bake in the preheated oven for about 12–15 minutes until the edges are just beginning to turn golden brown. The joy of these cookies is their slightly doughy texture, so you don't want to overcook them.

Let cool on the sheets for a few minutes to firm up, then use a palette knife or similar to transfer them to a wire rack but be very careful when you do this because they will be extremely fragile until they cool completely. Eat them as soon as they are cool enough to handle, and wash them down with a large mug of tea. *If* you have any left over (it's unlikely!), they will keep for a good few days in an airtight container.

))) Tropical Fruit Salad with Chilli & Lime Syrup (right)

This is a fantastic twist on fresh fruit salad. Serve it on its own or with a dollop of ice cream.

3 kiwi fruit, peeled and cut
    into thin discs
1 small pineapple, peeled,
    cored and cut into thin discs
1 ripe mango, cut into strips
small handful of fresh mint
    leaves, very finely chopped
drizzle of honey

Chilli & lime syrup

freshly squeezed juice of
    1 lime, plus extra to finish
½ Aji Limo chilli (this is quite
    hot with a distinct lemony
    flavour)
60 g/⅓ cup unrefined caster
    sugar/raw cane sugar

Serves 4–6

Pat the kiwi and pineapple dry with kitchen paper/paper towels. To make the chilli & lime syrup, put 60 ml/¼ cup water, the lime juice and chilli in a non-stick frying pan and heat gently for 5–10 minutes, stirring frequently. Test for chilli heat – if it is not strong enough, infuse over low heat until the heat meets your requirements. Remove the chilli. Add the sugar and stir. Heat, shaking the pan frequently to prevent the syrup from sticking to the bottom, until the sugar has dissolved. Now let it bubble gently for 6–8 minutes until it starts to turn slightly golden. Put a piece of kiwi on a fork and dip into the pan. Cook in the syrup for 45 seconds each side. Repeat with the remaining kiwi and pineapple pieces, setting them aside in a large bowl while you cook the rest. To the large bowl add all the remaining ingredients and a dash of lime.

> **RECOMMENDED CHILLIES:** If you can't find Aji Limo, use a reduced amount of hot, fruity Habanero or Scotch Bonnet.

))) Dried Fruit Salad with Ginger Mascarpone Cream

This makes a tasty and unusual conclusion to any meal but it's also good for breakfast with plain yogurt.

300 g/2 generous cups mixed
    dried fruit, eg pear, apple,
    apricots and prunes
200 ml/¾ cup apple juice
5 tablespoons syrup from
    a jar of stem ginger
1 star anise
1 whole dried Cayenne chilli,
    split

Ginger mascarpone cream

150 ml/⅔ cup whipping cream
250 g/1 cup mascarpone
3–4 pieces of stem ginger,
    very finely chopped

Serves 4–6

Put the dried fruit, apple juice, 4 tablespoons of the ginger syrup, the star anise and chilli into a heavy-based saucepan, cover and bring to a gentle simmer. Simmer over the lowest heat, covered, for at least 1½ hours, or until nearly all the moisture has been absorbed. Remove from the heat and let infuse overnight. Dried fruit varies in moisture content so you may need to add more juice during the cooking process. The fruit should rehydrate to become as juicy as possible.

Make the ginger mascarpone cream the next day. Put the whipping cream into a large mixing bowl and whisk until light and fluffy. Gently fold in the mascarpone, remaining ginger syrup and the ginger pieces until well mixed. Bring the salad to room temperature, remove the star anise and chilli, and serve with the ginger mascarpone cream.

> **RECOMMENDED CHILLIES:** Cayenne – we've used a dried Joe's Long.

Mulled Cider with Pasilla Chilli & Star Anise (left)

Having grown up in the southwest of England, it would be remiss of me not to include a recipe featuring cider. I remember being introduced to mulled cider at Glastonbury Festival in the mid nineties. I wasn't very hopeful when I was handed the cloudy orange liquid but it hit the spot and several glasses later I had forgotten all about the rain and cold. I subsequently found out it was 'local' cider at 12% ABV! Do use traditional-style farmhouse cider rather than the crystal clear brewery fizz for this recipe!

1 litre/4 cups (hard) cider
500 ml/2 cups apple juice
1–2 tablespoons honey or more
4 star anise
4 whole cloves
2 cinnamon sticks
1 dried Pasilla chilli, cut into strips

Put all the ingredients in a large saucepan and heat gently for at least 15 minutes to allow the flavours to infuse, but don't allow to boil. Strain the cider through a fine sieve/strainer before serving.

> **RECOMMENDED CHILLIES:** Dried Pasilla chillies are widely available online; they are mild, with hints of raisin and tobacco. If you can't get these, I would recommend Ancho or even Mulato dried chillies as a substitute.

Makes 6–8 cups

Spicy Mulled Wine

Many years ago I found myself in Venice a short time before Christmas. I know there are many worse places to be, but things had not been going particularly well and I was beginning to wish I was back home. Some Italian friends persuaded me to go to a preview evening in a rather stately gallery next to the Grand Canal. I had the best mulled wine I had ever tasted and if it taught me anything it was to take an interest in everything. You never know where you are going to end up or how useful it may turn out to be!

300 ml/1¼ cups pressed (pure) apple juice
200 g/1 cup vanilla sugar
freshly squeezed juice of 1 orange
grated zest of 1 lemon
1 small lime, halved
stick of cinnamon
2 cardamom pods, bruised
1 whole dried Cayenne chilli
2 fresh bay leaves
whole nutmeg, for grating
6 allspice berries
2 bottles of red wine
2 star anise

Put the apple juice, sugar, orange juice, lemon zest, lime halves, cinnamon, cardamom, chilli, bay leaves, 12–15 fresh gratings of nutmeg and the allspice berries in a saucepan. Heat gently, stirring constantly, until the sugar has dissolved. Now simmer for 10–15 minutes to infuse the syrup with the flavours of the various spices. The mixture should significantly reduce during this stage to create a rich syrup, but add a little water if it becomes too thick.

Add the wine and the star anise. Gently reheat, being careful not to boil. Strain the mulled wine before serving.

MY TIP: To make your own vanilla sugar; place a used (deseeded) vanilla pod/bean into a large jar of sugar and infuse for several days.

Makes 10–12 glasses

 # Chilli Chai

I love chai – it's perfect when you need a mid-morning boost and can't possibly stomach another cup of coffee! Chai is essentially black tea infused with spices and served with lots of sweetened warm milk. There are literally infinite variations, and this recipe should only be regarded as a starting point. Enjoy playing around with the recipe to come up with your own perfect blend. Also, once you have your own signature spice blend, mix up a large batch and scoop into empty jam jars for great homemade gifts. Allowing the milk to reach boiling point is an integral part of making authentic chai, even though it seems to go against everything we were ever taught about heating milk!

2–3-cm/1-inch piece of fresh ginger, finely sliced

2 star anise

1 fresh bay leaf

8 cardamom pods, bruised

6 whole cloves

3-cm/1¼-inch piece of cinnamon stick

2.5 cm/1 inch of vanilla pod/ bean

1 dried Cayenne or Zimbabwe Bird chilli

250 ml/1 cup milk

1½ tablespoons honey

1 tablespoon loose black tea leaves, or 2 strong teabags

Makes 2 cups

Put 500 ml/2 cups water into a small, heavy-based saucepan and add the ginger, star anise, bay leaf, cardamom, cloves, cinnamon, vanilla and chilli. Bring to the boil, then turn the heat down to achieve a gentle simmer. Simmer for about 10 minutes to allow the spices to infuse the water.

Add the milk and honey to the pan and bring to the boil for a brief moment before turning down the heat again to a gentle simmer.

Add the tea and simmer for 2 minutes before removing from the heat. Let stand for a further 2 minutes before straining into cups with a tea strainer.

> **RECOMMENDED CHILLIES:** Dried Cayenne, Zimbabwe Bird, Zanzibar or Bird's Eye

))))) Chilli Hot Chocolate

My wife was recently taken ghyll (ravine)-scrambling on a fairly bleak day in a particularly wind-swept part of Northumberland. She is not an especially outdoorsy-type by nature, nor is she that brave when it comes to heights, or icy water, especially if she has to jump from one into the other. However, having survived the experience, on returning to the minibus she was handed a steaming cup of chilli hot chocolate, which I have on good authority is the only way to truly, truly appreciate quite how delicious this drink is. After all, the Aztecs did consider this to be food (or rather drink) of the Gods.

500 ml/2 cups whole milk (or semi-skimmed if that is your preference, but personally I don't think you should skimp with hot chocolate)

60 g/2 oz. dark/bittersweet chocolate, grated

½ nutmeg, grated (or ½ teaspoon ground nutmeg)

1 dried Cayenne chilli, cut in half lengthways and deseeded

sugar, to taste

double/heavy cream, to swirl on top (optional, although it ought not to be…)

Makes 2–4 cups

Pour the milk into a small, heavy-based saucepan and add the grated chocolate, nutmeg and chilli. Heat very gently over low heat, making sure the milk doesn't boil and stirring occasionally to help melt the chocolate.

When the chocolate has completely melted and doesn't look at all grainy, continue to heat until tiny bubbles are just starting to appear around the edges of the pan. Turn off the heat, carefully remove the two halves of dried Cayenne and pour the hot chocolate into 2 large or 4 smaller cups. Add sugar to taste and finish off with a swirl of double/heavy cream.

RECOMMENDED CHILLIES: Any medium-heat chilli.

)))) The Perfect Bloody Mary

This has always been my favourite cocktail but nearly everywhere I sampled one I came away slightly disappointed. The only answer was to create my own! Along with my friend Owen we have tweaked (and re-tweaked) this recipe over the past decade until I think we have got pretty close to perfection. It is spicy and refreshing at the same time, with a lovely balance of sweet, savoury, sharp and spicy notes. I have tried adding other ingredients but I always come back to this. This is the perfect welcome drink for any summer get-together; and if you have drawn the short straw the mixer itself makes a delicious alcohol-free cocktail.

seeds from 1 small cardamom pod (no more than 3–4 seeds)

¼–½ teaspoon black peppercorns

250 ml/1 cup high-quality passata (Italian strained tomatoes) or organic tomato juice

2 tablespoons Tamari soy sauce (or other soy sauce)

2 teaspooons Claret or other dry red wine

1 tablespoon agave nectar

freshly squeezed juice of 1 lemon

½ teaspoon paprika

½ teaspoon celery seeds

½ Habanero chilli, deseeded and finely chopped

¼ teaspoon ground allspice

¼ teaspoon horseradish purée

½ teaspoon sea salt

To serve
ice cubes
100 ml/3½ oz. vodka
2 celery sticks, elegantly trimmed

Makes 2

Roughly grind together the cardamom seeds and peppercorns with a pestle and mortar.

Put in a food processor with all the other ingredients and blend until smooth and fully combined. Pour into a bottle or jug/pitcher, cover and leave for several hours to allow the flavours to infuse and mingle.

To serve, put ice into 2 tall glasses. In each glass add half the vodka and half the tomato juice mixture. Mix with a trimmed stick of celery!

MY TIP: Take the half Habanero chilli from the tip of the chilli, as this is likely to be slightly less hot – you can always add more later, or even a dash of hot sauce.

> RECOMMENDED CHILLIES: Any Habanero will be ideal.

Suppliers & Stockists

UK

This is a small representation of the wealth of chilli outlets and farms now doing business in the UK. For more information on the full range of UK suppliers why not visit www.chilefoundry.co.uk

Chillipepperpete

Run by Pete Seymour and his family, Chilli Pepper Pete and Fiery Foods UK offer an astonishingly broad range of chilli products from seeds and dried chillies (a really extensive range) through hot sauces and curry sauces to chilli gifts and treats. They also host the Fiery Foods chilli festivals in the UK and organise the UK National Chilli Awards. Busy people!
www.chillipepperpete.com

Edible Ornamentals

Edible Ornamentals, based in Bedfordshire, operate the UK's first 'Pick your own' chilli. In season, over 40 varieties of chilli are available to pick fresh. Both fresh chillies and plants and an exciting range of their own products are also available from their online shop.
www.edibleornamentals.co.uk

Hot Headz

Run by Stuart McAllister, Hot Headz was the first specialist chilli retailer in the UK. They operate an excellent website selling not only their own products but a great range of sauces, salsas and chilli products from all over the world. Their smoked chilli and garlic hot sauce is one of my favourite chilli products ever!
www.hot-headz.com

Nicky's Nursery

Suppliers of an excellent and broad range of chilli seeds. They sell in excess of 200 varieties of chilli seeds via their website and I have found them to provide some of the most reliable seeds I have ever bought. In 2008 and 2009 Which awarded them a "Which Best Buy", further enhancing their reputation for quality.
www.nickys-nursery.co.uk

Scorchio.co.uk

Now the UK's leading online chilli deli with a monstrous range of products from the UK and around the world. Loads to choose from and great service!
www.scorchio.co.uk

Sea Spring Seeds

Run by Joy and Michael Michaud, Sea Spring Seeds sell an extremely well trialled and selective range of chilli seeds. They also operate Sea Spring Plants and Peppers by Post selling chilli pug plants and fresh chillies respectively. Sea Spring is the home to the now legendary Dorset Naga.
www.seaspringseeds.co.uk

Seasoned Pioneers

Endorsed by leading food writers and offering without doubt the most comprehensive range of specialist spice blends and seasonings available in the UK, Seasoned Pioneers are true to their word and represent every major worldwide cuisine and an awful lot that are not so major! If any spice, herb or blend is proving particularly elusive this is always my first port of call.
www.seasonedpioneers.co.uk

Simpson's Seeds

Located on the Longleat Estate in Wiltshire, Simpson's Seeds provide a great range of chilli seeds from their own nursery. Matt Simpson has also written an excellent book on growing chillies: Chilli, Chili, Chile: Peppers Sweet and Hot. The nursery is open from April each year but their seed shop is open all year round. Seeds can also be purchased from their website.
www.simpsonsseeds.co.uk

South Devon Chilli Farm

Opened in 2003, South Devon Chilli Farm is run by Jason Nickels and Steve Waters. Over 2 sites they grow in excess of 10,000 chilli plants per year. Their Loddiswell site has a small shop open 7 days a week. They also have an excellent online shop which sells a broad range of their products, including fresh chillies from July to November.
www.southdevonchillifarm.co.uk

Spicy Monkey

Handmade curry pastes, spice mixes and marinades from northeast England – the spiritual home of chilli!
www.spicymonkey.co.uk

The Chile Seed Company

Founded and run by Gerald Fowler, this Cumbrian-based business sells an extraordinary array of chilli seeds as well a good range of their own products. They can also be found at nearly any UK event with chilli in the title!
www.chileseeds.co.uk

The Chilli Jam Man

Simon makes a wonderful range of chilli jams (as the name suggests). Made with great passion and enthusiasm, they are some of the best British chilli products out there.
www.thechillijamman.com

Trees Can't Dance

Obviously my favourite UK chilli company! Lovingly hand-crafted range of chilli goodies. We started with the world's most northerly chilli farm and although things have grown, we still make everything by hand at our bespoke production kitchen in Northumberland. If you haven't tried our products yet, please give them a go – you really don't know what you are missing!
www.treescantdance.co.uk

Upton Cheyney Chilli Farm

One of my favourite new chilli companies. Located between Bath and Bristol, their growing and manufacture really embrace the field to fork ethos! They even hold their own chilli festival on the farm at the beginning of September.
www.uptonchilli.co.uk

Wiltshire Chilli Farm

As with most great ideas, Wiltshire Chilli Farm was dreamt up in the pub. They are a relative newcomer in the UK, having started growing chillies in February 2010. They have grown quickly and now operate from 4200sq ft of growing space. They will be offering fresh chillies for sale from summer 2012.
www.justchillies.co.uk/wiltshirechillies

US

Kalustyan's

Online groceries, including a huge range of dried chillies, spices, ground peppers and more. Eg sweet smoked paprika (pimentón dulce) and Piquillo peppers.
www.kalustyans.com

La Tienda

Stockists of the best Spanish produce including fresh Padron peppers, roasted Piquillo peppers and sweet smoked paprika (pimentón dulce).
www.tienda.com

Marx Foods

Mostly commercial supplier, but they have a good stock of fresh, dried and ground/crushed chillies.
www.marxfoods.com

Melissa's

Great source for hard-to-find fresh produce including dozens of different chillies.
www.melissas.com

New Mexican Connection

For all fresh and dried New Mexican favourites.
www.newmexicanconnection.com

Penzeys Spices

Ground Ancho, smoked Chipotles, Piquin, galangal, and all manner of spices, herbs and seasonings.
www.penzeys.com

Tierra Vegetables

Brother and sister Wayne and Lee James have been farming 20 acres in the heart of the Sonoma Country Wine Country, 70 miles north of San Francisco, since 1979. In addition to growing a market garden, they also grow more than 20 varieties of chillies and sweet peppers. They also sell dried chillies.
www.tierravegetables.com

World Spice

Seattle's premier spice, herb and tea shop with a great online collection of whole or ground dried spices, including Piment d'Espelette. They also stock dried Mexican oregano, Baharat spice blend and Ras el Hanout.
www.worldspice.com

Index

acknowledgments

People who without which…
Becky, for loving living in a house that
always smells of chilli and for adding
so much to these recipes; Freddie,
Theo and Ella, for giving me an honest
perspective on everything and for
trying things they were sure they
wouldn't like! Owen, Michelle and the
girls, for always providing help when
I need it, still being enthusiastic about
everything and not visibly flinching
when I say 'I've had a brilliant idea';
Jamie C, for answering stupid queries
and not actually laughing out loud;
John, Christine and Jamie at TCD, for
supporting this idea and listening
to me blather on ceaselessly about
chillies for the past 5 years; Patrick,
Katharina, Geoff, Athene and Tim, for
accepting that I never know what I
will be doing tomorrow let alone in
6 months' time; Céline, Julia, Steve
and everyone else at RPS, who made
writing this an (almost) completely
painless process; Jane Milton and her
girls, who tested the recipes; Peter, for
the amazing photography; Keith Floyd,
Rick Stein, Hugh F-W, Simon Majumdar
and Kenny Atkinson, for providing
inspiration; and finally my mum, who,
despite everything, ensured I knew
how to cook, and my Dad, who always
ate everything I made for him.